# THE MULTILATERAL DEVELOPMENT BANKS

## VOLUME 4
## THE INTER-AMERICAN DEVELOPMENT BANK

# THE MULTILATERAL DEVELOPMENT BANKS ⸻

## VOLUME 4

# THE INTER-AMERICAN DEVELOPMENT BANK

### DIANA TUSSIE

LYNNE RIENNER PUBLISHERS

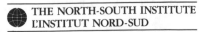

THE NORTH-SOUTH INSTITUTE
L'INSTITUT NORD-SUD

Published in the United States of America in 1995 by
Lynne Rienner Publishers, Inc.
1800 30th Street, Boulder, Colorado 80301

and in the United Kingdom by
Lynne Rienner Publishers, Inc.
3 Henrietta Street, Covent Garden, London WC2E 8LU

Paperback edition published in Canada by
The North-South Institute
55 Murray Street
Ottawa, Ontario K1N 5M3 Canada

**Library of Congress Cataloging-in-Publication Data**
Multilateral development banks.
   p.   cm.
   Includes bibliographical references and index.
      Contents: — 4. The Inter-American Development Bank  /  by Diana Tussie.
      ISBN 1-55587-466-5 (alk. paper  :  v. 4)—
      ISBN 1-55587-492-4 (pbk.  :  alk. paper  :  v. 4)
      1. Development banks. 2. Inter-American Development Bank.
   HG1975.M848  1995
   332.2—dc20
                                                              94-45003
                                                              CIP

**Canadian Cataloguing in Publication Data**
Main entry under title:
Multilateral Development Banks
   Includes bibliographical references.
      Contents: v. 4. The Inter-American Development Bank  /  by Diana Tussie.
      ISBN 0-921942-83-4 (v.4) (pbk)
      1. Development banks. I. North-South Institute (Ottawa, Ont.)
   HG1975.M85  1995  332.1'52 C95-900188-3

**British Cataloguing in Publication Data**
A Cataloguing in Publication record for this book
is available from the British Library.


Printed and bound in the United States of America

   The paper used in this publication meets the requirements
∞ of the American National Standard for Permanence of
   Paper for Printed Library Materials Z39.48-1984.

 5  4  3  2  1

As the Lion King would have it,
for Ximena and Natalia,
for the circle of life, forever.

૨૭

"We have no more right to consume
happiness without producing it,
than to consume wealth without producing it."
—George Bernard Shaw, *Candida*

# CONTENTS

# TABLES AND FIGURES

## Tables

## Figures

# FOREWORD

This well-researched study brings out the considerable difficulties faced by the Inter-American Development Bank in striking a politically adequate and technically effective balance among several internal and external objectives, claims, factors, and forces. These objectives have changed dramatically since the 1960s, when the Bank started operations, to the 1990s, as it enters a new stage.

The IDB is faced with the need to overcome the weaknesses and take advantage of the strengths of the past, while adapting to radically different circumstances. These circumstances require moving into the uncharted and sensitive ground of program lending and policy reform in a new partnership with the World Bank and the International Monetary Fund. In this process, it is essential for the IDB to conserve and strengthen the special relationship that it has developed with its regional borrowing member countries, particularly the smaller ones, in terms of mutual understanding, intellectual leadership, and policy dialogue.

The shift in orientation brings with it new tasks. These include lending to the private sector, especially for the development of small and microenterprises; supporting new and intensified policies, programs, and activities for the alleviation of poverty and inequality; helping with institutional reforms aimed at increased responsiveness and accountability of smaller but more effective governments; contributing to the resumption of investment and growth while strengthening competitiveness and environmental concerns; and cooperating with the renewed enthusiasm for regional economic integration. The Bank's resources and capabilities, and its supporting regional networks, must be deployed with a keen sense of priorities in order to be effective in both the short and the long term.

The Inter-American Development Bank has strong roots in the Latin American region and a praiseworthy tradition of sharing its interests and evolution. It also has a positive record of submitting itself willingly to external reviews and evaluations and of responding to recommendations. The findings of this study are highly relevant and should be weighed carefully at a time when the IDB is undertaking a major reorganization to adjust to a new agenda.

I would like to express my appreciation to the North-South Institute for undertaking its project on multilateral development banks and, reflecting my regional bias, particularly for Diana Tussie's outstanding study of the IDB. The development community owes the institute and Roy Culpeper, its vice president and project director, its gratitude for a significant and timely contribution to the understanding of key institutions of international cooperation.

*Osvaldo Sunkel*
President
Corporación de Investigaciones para el Desarrollo

# PREFACE

In 1991 the North-South Institute launched its research project on the multilateral development banks ("the MDB Project"). The principal focus of the project was the group of regional development banks (comprising the African, Asian, and Inter-American Development Banks) plus the subregional Caribbean Development Bank. All these banks, created more or less in the image of the World Bank, had been around for two to three decades. Yet, in contrast to the World Bank, they had been subjected to little critical scrutiny.

The project was designed to provide a consistent framework for examining each of the banks. Besides providing a brief history of the origins and evolution of its subject, each study reviews the experience of a selected group of borrowing countries, as well as the bank's performance as a lender and as a mobilizer of resources. In all of the studies, the operations and policies of the regional bank are compared with the World Bank; also addressed are relations between the two agencies and the division of labor between them. Finally, each study looks ahead at the challenges facing the banks in the future.

In a word, the studies seek to determine the *development effectiveness* of the regional banks by examining their impact on growth, poverty, the environment, and social indicators of development. It is hoped that the project will contribute to ongoing discussions regarding the future of the multilateral system of development financing, now in its fiftieth year after the Bretton Woods Conference. In addition to this volume on the Inter-American Bank, the project will yield four other major publications—one each on the Asian, Caribbean, and African Banks, as well as a "synthesis" volume. There are also two studies on Canada's role in the MDBs, one on Sweden and the MDBs, and one on Jamaica's relations with the MDBs.

The project has been generously supported through grants from the Canadian International Development Agency, the Inter-American Development Bank, the Asian Development Bank, the African Development Bank, the Ford Foundation, the Swedish Ministry for Foreign Affairs, the Caribbean Development Bank, the Norwegian

Ministry of Foreign Affairs, and the Netherlands Ministry for Development Cooperation. The views contained in each volume, however, are those of the author alone and do not necessarily reflect the views of the project's sponsors, the funders of the multilateral development banks project, the North-South Institute, its supporters, or its board of directors.

*Roy Culpeper*
MDB Project Director
The North-South Institute

# ACKNOWLEDGMENTS

The most gratifying, but also the most humbling, part of researching and writing a book is to sit down at the end of the process and acknowledge the many debts incurred along the way.

This book is part of a larger project on the regional development banks directed by the North-South Institute. My thanks are due to the North-South Institute for giving me the opportunity to participate in the project and particularly to Roy Culpeper, director of the project. His persistent questioning and meticulous reading of various drafts have been the single most important contribution in determining the direction I have taken. My thanks also to Sarah Matthews and Andrew Clark at the institute, who were generous in answering my endless requests from Ottawa to Buenos Aires, and to Clyde Sanger and Rowena Beamish for their editing. My colleagues on the team, Nihal Kappagoda and Chandra Hardy (authors of *The Asian Development Bank* and *The Caribbean Development Bank*), have also shared their knowledge generously and made important suggestions. The advisory board, comprising Jonathan Frimpong-Ansah, Catherine Gwin, John Lewis, Saburo Okita (until his death in February 1993, when he was succeeded by Yasutami Shimomura), Jean Quesnel, and Miguel Urrutia (who withdrew in July 1993 and was replaced by Osvaldo Sunkel), guided the study of all the regional development banks, provided valuable counsel, and made suggestions for improvement.

I wish to acknowledge the extensive cooperation provided by the Inter-American Development Bank during the research for this study. Without the enthusiasm of Enrique Iglesias and Nohra Rey de Marulanda, it would not have been possible. Daniel Szabo deserves particular mention for coordinating my visits to the Bank and for helping me through the maze. Many staff members and executive directors discussed aspects of the Bank's work and shared their expertise. I wish to thank particularly Andres Bajuk, Ciro de Falco, Eloy Garcia, Richard Fletcher, Richard Herring, Elio Londero, Ann Morales, Humberto Petrei, Alberto Pico, Luis Ratinoff, William Robinson, Luis Rubio, Charles Skeete, and William McWhinney. Ira Kaylin and Hector Luisi showed patience with simple questions. I owe a very special debt to the field offices in Buenos Aires and Chile where this study was written. Paul Kohling and José Maria Puppo opened doors and shared their insights. In Buenos Aires, Margarita Ryan was invaluable in tracking documentation.

I have also benefited from the cooperation of several officers at the World Bank. I wish to thank in particular Carlos Quijano among the many people who gave me a perspective on the relationship among the banks.

The case studies in the book draw on research provided by Ennio Rodriguez for Costa Rica and Gonzalo Chavez for Bolivia. Maria Wagner, Nicole Moussa, Guillermo Canovas, and my daughter Ximena Federman provided research assistance at different stages. I am grateful to many others who took time to advise and counsel me. Arturo O'Connell deserves special mention, as do Mirta Botzman and Luciano Tomassini. My participation in a study coordinated by Stephany Griffith-Jones gave me further insights and new perspectives.

*Diana Tussie*

# ACRONYMS

| | |
|---|---|
| AfDB | African Development Bank |
| AfDF | African Development Fund (of AfDB) |
| AsDB | Asian Development Bank |
| AsDF | Asian Development Fund (of AsDB) |
| BEP | borrowers' ex post evaluations |
| BMCs | borrowing member countries |
| CACM | Central American Common Market |
| CBI | Caribbean Basin Initiative |
| CDB | Caribbean Development Bank |
| CPP | country programming paper |
| DDSR | debt or debt service reduction |
| DES | Department of Economic and Social Affairs (IDB) |
| DFI | development financing institution |
| DPL | Department of Plans and Programs (IDB) |
| EAI | Enterprise for the Americas Initiative |
| EBRD | European Bank for Reconstruction and Development |
| ECLAC | Economic Commission for Latin America and the Caribbean |
| EFF | enhanced financing facility |
| ENLACE | Entidad Latinoamericana Cientifico Empresarial (Latin American Scientific and Entrepreneurial Entity) |
| ESAF | Enhanced Structural Adjustment Facility |
| ESF | Emergency Social Fund (Bolivia) |
| ESF | Economic Support Fund (Costa Rica) |
| FSO | Fund for Special Operations (IDB) |
| GAO | Government Accounting Office (U.S.) |
| GCI | general capital increase |
| GDP | gross domestic product |
| GNP | gross national product |
| GRI | general resource increase |
| ICE | Instituto Costaricence de Electricidad |
| IDA | International Development Association (World Bank) |
| IDB | Inter-American Development Bank |

| | |
|---|---|
| IFC | International Finance Corporation (World Bank) |
| IFF | Intermediate Financing Facility (IDB) |
| IFI | international financial institution |
| IIC | Inter-American Investment Corporation (IDB affiliate) |
| ILPES | Instituto Latinoamericano de Planificación Económica y Social |
| IMF | International Monetary Fund |
| ISL | investment sector loan |
| JSF | Japan Special Fund |
| LAFTA | Latin American Free Trade Association |
| MDB | multilateral development bank |
| MIF | Multilateral Investment Fund |
| NAFTA | North American Free Trade Agreement |
| NEP | New Economic Policy (Bolivia, 1985) |
| NGO | nongovernmental organization |
| OAS | Organization of American States |
| OC | ordinary capital |
| OEO | operations evaluation office (IDB) |
| ORE | office of review and evaluation (IDB) |
| PCR | project completion report |
| PFP | policy framework paper |
| PPF | Project Preparation Facility |
| PSRL | public sector reform loan (Argentina) |
| RDB | regional development bank |
| SAF | Structural Adjustment Facility (IMF) |
| SAL | structural adjustment loan |
| SECAL | sectoral adjustment loan |
| SLL | sustainable level of lending |
| SPTF | Social Progress Trust Fund |
| TAPOMA | task force on portfolio management |
| UNDP | United Nations Development Programme |
| USAID | U.S. Agency for International Development |
| WHFTA | Western Hemisphere Free Trade Area |
| WID | women in development |

# 1

# INTRODUCTION

For Latin America and parts of the Caribbean, the Inter-American Development Bank (IDB) is the leading development institution today. Since its creation in 1959 the IDB has become a source of financial, technical, and intellectual resources to the region, although its specific contribution has varied from country to country and from period to period.

As a regional development institution it has developed a special relationship with its borrowing member countries (BMCs). BMCs have held the majority of the Bank's capital resources and voting shares. In fact, the IDB's Articles of Agreement now stipulate that the voting power of the BMCs cannot fall below 50.005 percent of the total. This share stood at 53.5 percent until 1994, at which time its articles were amended to allow Japan, Germany, Italy, and France to increase their respective stakes. The president of the Bank has always come from a borrowing member country. The vision of a regional development bank rested precisely on the creation of an institution in which control remained largely in the hands of the BMCs. The goal was to counter the perceived marginalization of the region by the Bretton Woods institutions in which voting power was heavily weighted in favor of the industrial countries. The IDB's mission was to emphasize a different voice.

The structure of the IDB's governance has given the BMCs a strong sense of entitlement and commitment to the Bank. Because of its regional provenance, the Bank can inspire and guide, rather than impose, policy reforms. Even when the goals are agreed upon, process and style are important. The IDB can make the donor's agenda compatible with national and regional sensitivities; it can then evaluate the region's agenda and make it presentable for funding.

This sense of trust and ownership is an important feature of a regional development bank, but it is not sufficient to justify its existence. Its raison d'être must be proven. This book tries to point out the individuality of the IDB by analyzing the evolution of its lending program and its division of labor with the World Bank. It concentrates on the period from 1970 to the early 1990s, although the Bank's inaugural decade is touched on to put contemporary issues in perspective and to understand the Bank's changing role.

The individuality of the IDB has stemmed more from its corporate culture and its small country focus than from sectoral differentiation or specific types of loans. One of the most noticeable trends in the Bank's lending program has been the steady concentration of concessional funding (from the Fund for Special Operations) among the dozen poorest and smallest countries in the region. Their share of total concessional funds rose from 30 percent in the 1970–1972 period to an average of 86 percent in 1988–1990. Over the two decades these countries received an average of 60 percent of the concessional funds.

The analysis concludes that, as the threat of the debt crisis of the 1980s has ebbed, BMCs now place renewed demands on the Bank. If there were not an IDB, many regional developing countries would labor to create it, although it would probably look different from the one we have today. Not only has the international climate changed dramatically in the past decades, but BMCs have new priorities and so do nonborrowing members. The IDB must prepare itself to face the end of the millennium with a new Weltanschauung.

## The Contribution of the Inter-American Development Bank in Historical Perspective

The idea of a regional development bank (RDB) goes back to the end of the nineteenth century, but it took over sixty years to come to fruition. The IDB was an offspring of the state-led vision of development that bloomed in Latin America in the 1950s, a vision pioneered by Raul Prebisch and the Economic Commission for Latin America (ECLA), later to become the Economic Commission for Latin America and the Caribbean (ECLAC). In a nutshell, the structuralist school of thought argued that Latin America faced foreign exchange bottlenecks due to the structure of its exports. In addition, domestic economies were characterized by a weak private sector and insufficient capital. The market failures were used to justify strong state leadership and import-substituting industrialization. The IDB was established as a crucial link in resource transfers.

The IDB's early years coincided with a time when the world economy experienced unparalleled expansion, but the access of developing countries to capital markets was far from extensive. The Bank was founded to bridge that gap. The first IDB loans were in housing, sanitation, and education, thus accepting financing challenges in sectors that were not necessarily viewed as "bankable" in international banking circles. The success of its first decade has been well documented (Calvo and Tomassini 1970; Dell 1972; White 1970) and praised widely. It gained from the momentum created by President Kennedy's "Alliance for Progress" and a contribution of $525 million to the IDB's Social Progress Trust Fund (SPTF) in 1961. The United States was then the sole "net" donor country and held 42.05 percent of the voting power. Relations between the governments of Latin America and the United States were, on the whole, cordial. The U.S. administrations in the 1960s were comparatively interventionist. At the same time, the prevailing development model throughout much of Latin America was a variant of a statist, largely inward-oriented, import substitution model. As the country studies show, IDB programs gave overall support to the state-led development model and endorsed social intervention.

The Bank thus established for itself a reputation as the "water and sanitation bank," because it was the major provider of external funding for this sector. It was also known as the "university bank" because of its loans and assistance to institutions of higher learning and the "integration bank" because of its support for regional economic integration. These indicate the diversified activities that have characterized its mandate and its functions.

The United States remained the region's single most important partner in trade and investment, but the Bank sought other sources of funding as the distribution of global economic power changed. The admission of Canada and nonregional, nonborrowing countries in 1973 increased the Bank's potential for resource mobilization and enhanced its multilateral character. This was also a time when the hemispheric consensus that had inspired the Alliance for Progress reached a low ebb (Iglesias 1992). On the one hand, the governments in various Latin American countries, some of them military, took more independent or nationalistic stances. On the other, the inauguration of President Richard Nixon in 1969 led to a change in U.S. foreign policy priorities. Its agenda became more global and less oriented to its own hemisphere.

By this time conditions in international capital markets were dramatically transformed. The successive oil shocks of the 1970s were accompanied by a period of financial permissiveness and excessive borrowing from private sources. Current account deficits escalated as concern for development theories and strategies waned. "Everything seemed solvable through external financing" (Sunkel 1993, 32). Toward the end of the 1970s orthodox views prevailed in the region, particularly in the Southern Cone. The Bank's power in the overall development of the region diminished.[1] It was still significant in certain sectors, such as energy and sanitation, and it remained important for smaller, less-creditworthy economies of the region.

In the 1980s Latin America entered into its most severe, longest, and most widespread crisis. Interest rates escalated and overall international financial conditions deteriorated, wreaking havoc on borrowers. Credit became rationed. By the time the debt crisis erupted, Latin America's external debt was three times the value of its exports. The volume of exports expanded rapidly during the decade, but per capita incomes declined significantly. Income disparities worsened in almost all countries. The period is rightly known as "the lost decade." The region suffered a negative transfer of resources[2] of an average of $15–20 billion a year from 1983 to 1989. In 1989 it was equivalent to 10 percent of regional GDP.

The debt crisis also marked a downturn for the Bank. The IDB was not able to move rapidly to counteract the drying up of funds. As the focus changed from economic development to financial survival, the Bank lost its niche. Its very existence was questioned. These doubts precipitated a shift away from the Bank's traditional role in support of public sector investment programs to immediate balance-of-payments relief. This change came about only partly as a consequence of the perceived failures of public intervention; the real urgency was to avoid international financial collapse. The readjustment of objectives was difficult; Bank business was brought almost to a standstill in the course of acrimonious negotiations, which lasted almost three years from 1986 to 1989, the year of its Seventh Capital Replenishment.

The 1990s opened with a resurgence of international capital flows to the region triggered by declining interest rates in the United States, which fell to their lowest level in thirty years. The boom in private financial inflows accompanied a resumption of growth in many BMCs. In 1992 private capital inflows totaled $60 billion, over twice that of 1991 and six times that of 1990 (see Figure 1.1). Fiscal and trade policy reform, liberalization of foreign direct investment, and tighter monetary policies have encouraged capital inflows. Even countries that did not undertake these reforms, or undertook them only partially, experienced a turnaround in their inflows (Calvo et al. 1993). Yet massive inflows have also complicated the management of economic policy by appreciating exchange rates, increasing reserves, and swelling the money supply.

Thus the Bank has presided over successive periods of overlending and underlending from private capital markets, each bringing new challenges and requiring different types of counteractive measures, policy instruments, and lending modalities. The Bank has tried to play a compensatory role as it struggled with the market failures that characterized the development process.

**Figure 1.1    Latin America: Capital Flows, 1984–1992**

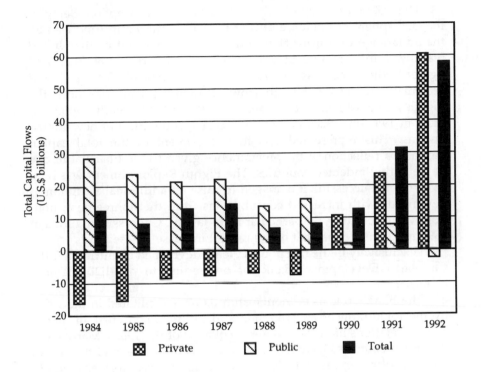

*Source:* IDB, *Economic and Social Progress in Latin America,* 1993.

The IDB is unique among all multilateral banks in having a built-in concessional window, the Fund for Special Operations (FSO) (Culpeper 1993). The creation of the FSO, predominantly for the region's poorest borrowing members, was simultaneous with the creation of the IDB and is an integral part of its juridical structure. At the Asian Development Bank and the African Development Bank, as well as in the World Bank, their concessional facilities were created after the banks themselves and operate as legally separate entities.[3]

As a result, contributions to the FSO must be agreed upon every four years in the context of "general resource increases," in contrast to the other banks, which hold separate replenishment negotiations for their hard and soft windows. This feature of the IDB has made replenishment negotiations protracted and all-encompassing exercises. All terms and contributions become part of a single undertaking and must be agreed upon simultaneously.

The FSO was exceptionally well endowed at inception. Being in the U.S. sphere of influence during the Cold War, Latin America had the advantage of a prior claim on U.S. transfers. But as the United States felt the pressure of wider interests and responsibilities and tighter budgets, concessional funds eroded drastically. The slack was not taken up by other nonborrowing member countries until the Eighth Replenishment, concluded in 1994. At the Seventh Replenishment in 1989 only $200 million was raised in the form of new contributions. This represented less than 1 percent of the total capital increase, a reflection of the preeminence given to the financial rescue of the highly indebted countries. The Eighth Replenishment was relatively more successful; it managed to raise an additional $1 billion in new funds with increased contributions from the nonregional, nonborrowing countries (in particular from Japan). Concessional funds in 1995 represent 2.5 percent of the capital increase. These funds will be used exclusively in the five poorest, least-developed countries and the Caribbean Development Bank for on-lending to non-IDB member countries.

The Bank's role as economic stimulator is facilitated in the 1990s by the rekindling of an economic and political consensus in hemispheric relations after the economic collapse of the 1980s. Many Latin American countries have returned to democratic rule, and the end of the Cold War has erased the ideological animosities of former times. In line with changes throughout the world, market-oriented policies have led to the freeing of trade, deregulation, and privatization. A new mindset has gained hold in the region, although some political and financial setbacks may be expected, as shown in Mexico with the uprisings in Chiapas, the murder of presidential candidate Daniel Colosio, and the collapse of the exchange rate in late 1994.

In many ways the spirit of hemispheric relations in the 1990s resembles that of the 1960s. The Bank and its president, Enrique Iglesias, are active champions of this vision. A hemispheric summit took place in 1994, the first since 1967. The creation of the North American Free Trade Agreement (NAFTA) is a beacon of hope, even if not the dawn of a bright new era for which many leaders had wished. If NAFTA spreads to the rest of the hemisphere, the Bank will have to become more involved in supporting adjustment to free trade in the BMCs. It will need to increase staff trained to analyze the needed adjustments and to provide technical assistance in the regulatory areas that are emerging for negotiation. It will have to ensure consistency of its social agenda as liberalized trade alters production and employment patterns. The different interests of nonregional, nonborrowing member countries may complicate this task.

The Bank's embrace of the U.S. "Enterprise for the Americas Initiative" (EAI) launched by President George Bush may be understood in this context. The EAI has three main components: the proposal to create a free trade area from Anchorage to Tierra del Fuego; a small facility to write off the public debt of countries to the United States; and the promotion of private investment within the hemisphere. This latter component has been the most important to date. It aims at the creation of a policy environment attractive to foreign investment and the return of flight capital. The investment component of the EAI has been placed in the hands of the IDB. To this end a Multilateral Investment Fund (MIF) has been created to provide technical assistance and support for private enterprise and for programs for human resource development.

## The Borrowing Member Countries

In order to guide access to resources from the Bank, BMCs were grouped into four categories known as A, B, C, and D according to their level of development, although some adjustments and political compromises were made in order to accommodate particular exigencies. Group A, which comprises Argentina, Brazil, Mexico, and Venezuela, held 36.84 percent of the voting power until 1993 and absorbed 55 percent of total lending in the 1961–1993 period. Venezuela as an oil exporter in the group was a relative latecomer to active borrowing from the Bank, starting only after the 1982 debt crisis.[4] Group B, which comprises Chile, Colombia, and Peru, holds 7.92 percent of the voting power. This group has received 19 percent of the Bank's total lending. Group C consists of the Bahamas, Barbados, Costa Rica, Jamaica, Trinidad and Tobago, and Uruguay. They have 3.18 percent of the voting power and have received 8 percent of total lending. Group D countries are the poorest, least-developed BMCs— Belize, Bolivia, the Dominican Republic, Ecuador, El Salvador, Guatemala, Guyana, Haiti, Honduras, Nicaragua, Panama, Paraguay, and Surinam. They have 5.82 percent of the voting power and have received nearly a quarter of all resources. As agreed during the Eighth Replenishment, the poorest of these, Bolivia, Guyana, Haiti, Honduras, and Nicaragua, will be the only countries entitled to soft loans in hard currencies from the FSO.

The IDB's largest borrowers have been the bigger economies in the region. Seventy percent of the Bank's disbursed loans are today concentrated in Brazil, Mexico, Argentina, Colombia, Chile, and Peru, which together account for 85 percent of regional GNP. Yet on a per capita basis, the Bank has lent more to the smaller and poorer countries. In its small BMCs—Group D—the IDB lends two to three times as much as the World Bank. For many of these small borrowers the Bank is the main external financial agent.

The Bank plays different roles in different countries. Its impact as a development institution has been more significant in the small BMCs. The bigger countries in the region have stronger institutional capabilities and a wider skills base, and they have historically had easier access to alternative sources of funds for their public sector investment programs. Here the Bank acts more as a financial intermediary than as a development agency. The small countries are more dependent on official development assistance and have greater manpower constraints. The impact of IDB funding is not only quantitative but also qualitative. The small countries need more guidance from the IDB and absorb relatively large amounts of lending and staff time. The IDB has been active in these countries in identifying opportunities, designing policies, and offering technical assistance.

As Jorge Quiroga, Bolivia's former minister of finance in 1992, expressed: When big countries like Mexico or Brazil shape up economically, they receive private investment. Countries like Bolivia need the IDB to be a catalytic element by lending directly to the private sector with government guarantees. For example, Bolivia has had massive gas export projects to Brazil and Chile that required IDB involvement.

This strategic bias toward the less-developed BMCs has been implemented via concessional loans and greater shares of nonreimbursable technical assistance. Policies also allow preferential treatment in the relative share of funds granted by the Bank for the total cost of a project. This distribution of Bank and counterpart funding is known as "the matrix." The matrix is graduated so that the least-developed countries can receive higher shares of Bank support than other BMCs per project.

While the economic performance of the region as a whole showed improvement starting in 1990, recovery in these countries remains fragile and tentative. In 1991 Haiti had the highest share of debt owed to multilateral sources in the region (58 percent), followed by Honduras (47 percent), Bolivia (42 percent), El Salvador (39 percent), and Guyana (27 percent). These figures reflect the limited access of these countries to alternative sources of funds and highlight the crucial role of the IDB.

Based on the small-country focus of the IDB and the danger of overlapping and duplication between the regional banks and the World Bank, there have been proposals for the World Bank to concentrate on the big countries where it has more clout and the regional banks to concentrate on the small countries where they have comparatively more knowledge and leverage. The arguments in favor of this division of labor are not totally persuasive in the case of the IDB. In the first place, the present cost structure of the IDB would not allow an exclusive concentration on its small BMCs. It is doubtful to what extent this emphasis on small countries could be maintained because of the high overhead costs of the Bank. The Bank's expenses are up to $1 million to prepare a loan; small loans below $50 million are not cost effective.[5]

To continue to lend to small countries and to become more efficient, the IDB will have to on-lend more funds to, and work out tighter arrangements with, the subregional banks: the Caribbean Development Bank, the Andean Development Fund, and the Central American Bank for Economic Integration. Together they cover the medium and small BMCs in the region. Moreover, the only countries not members of a subregional bank are the three largest: Argentina, Brazil, and Mexico,[6] as well as Chile, Uruguay, and Paraguay. Countries that receive massive private capital inflows could withdraw from active borrowing as Venezuela did during its oil bonanza. This could free resources for needier borrowers. A graduation policy to terminate the access of some countries to Bank loans could be flexible and reversible if a country again proved to be in need. It should be accompanied by a country risk analysis, particularly of the low-income, severely indebted countries, in order to take measures both to safeguard the quality of the Bank's portfolio and to adjust the flow of resources to BMCs according to their needs.

## The Way Forward

The efficiency of multilateral development banks is under fire from those who examine their administrative costs, staff benefits, or the magnificent buildings in which the banks are housed. These factors will increasingly come under scrutiny, and greater efficiency and transparency in these matters will be on the agenda of both nonborrowers and borrowers.

Multilateral development banks have a dual role as financial intermediaries and development institutions. They must operate financially as banks while maintaining a development perspective. There is great difficulty in striking the right balance between practicing sound lending and meeting development challenges. Yet the very complexity of the task makes a strong case for multilateralism. Poor and small countries suffer from pervasive credit rationing for which multilateral development banks can compensate. Multilateralism allows consistency and wider acceptance of objectives. Cassen et al. (1987) report that lack of coordination among bilateral donors is an important factor in the failure of aid to achieve its objectives.

A regional development bank may have a comparative advantage in this task. It is in a position to develop country-specific lending strategies that are closely in tune with the needs of each borrower. Moreover, as the policy dialogue extends into social and political fields, a regional development bank that embodies a degree of "ownership" by the Latin American and Caribbean countries is perhaps the most appropriate channel for this task—a task that requires urgent attention to the strengthening of institutions in this area and strong assistance for the mobilization of internal resources. The IDB's network of country offices, one in every BMC, is a key asset in this new mission. Created as agents for intensive technical assistance during project execution, country offices, although an integral part of the Bank, are sadly underutilized. In sum, the Bank must tap this potential source of institutional strength.

Felipe Herrera, the Bank's first president, claimed that the Bank should function as a "university of development," helping to elucidate ideas and proposals in support of economic modernization and development. The IDB is today bent on restoring this tradition. With the debt crisis easing and macroeconomic stability gaining ground, it is a good time for the germination of new ideas. The Bank's role as a catalyst for intellectual resources and policy advice is bound to accelerate as the Bank becomes a center for development thinking. The policy dialogue with borrowers is always a sensitive area, and it will become increasingly so as new areas, such as equity, environmental sustainability, and governance, are brought within its purview.

Latin America is recognized today as containing the worst income inequalities. Growth during the 1960s and 1970s did not reduce the number of poor, and the stagnation of the 1980s reversed much of the previous social progress that had been achieved. During this period, many countries' population growth outpaced the increases in housing, classrooms, jobs, and so on. The social effects of the debt crisis years have been devastating. There is evidence of persistent and growing inequality in the distribution of income in most BMCs (Cardoso and Helwege 1992). Moreover, the experience of the 1980s shows that in the absence of economic growth, the poor find it difficult to survive, let alone improve their lot. The experience of the 1960s and 1970s shows that growth is a necessary but insufficient condition to alleviate much of the region's poverty. Redistribution and targeted intervention are required.

This targeting requires careful planning, for the countries still have not been grouped into categories that correspond to their level of poverty in social as well as income terms. In addition, in the late 1970s and the 1980s poverty alleviation was less a concern than dealing with oil price rises and mounting national indebtedness. The experience of those years and the evidence of growing inequalities make it clear that the Bank has to place poverty efforts in the center of its work in every country. Measures to alleviate poverty have to be at the core of the Bank's strategy in every country, rather than only a part of its social program support.

Social reform is a process that works best from the bottom up. The Bank cannot be a substitute for domestic efforts, but it can and must be a catalyst. It is guiding a "second generation of socio-economic reforms" (IDB, "Economic and Social Progress in Latin America," 1993, 1), which would combine social equity with sustainable long-term growth. These reforms must focus on creating employment for the poor, stimulating investment in human resources and the urban environment, and improving the institutional, budgetary, and decision-making process in social sectors. Such efforts will not only improve the welfare of the poorest groups in the region on grounds of equity, they will enhance the sustainability of recent macroeconomic reforms, strengthen political stability, and contribute to the development of human resources, an essential ingredient for long-term growth.

Another major issue the IDB must resolve in its immediate future is the impact on its project pipeline of the widespread process of divestiture undertaken by its former clients. Since inception the IDB has functioned largely as an agency for financing public sector projects. However, its Articles of Agreement allow the Bank to make loans to private firms without government guarantees. To date, this has not been a major outlet for IDB activity. Private sector projects have been carried out with guarantees from the government. The Bank is addressing the implications of increased lending to the private sector on its portfolio quality, its financial base, its funding strategy, and its internal organization. This includes a revision of the mandate of its affiliate, the Inter-American Investment Corporation (IIC), which began operations in 1989 as an autonomous merchant banking corporation.

Even if capital inflows remain at present levels, such flows have historically been directed to the large, middle-income countries and to the large, more-established firms. The Bank must redouble its efforts to become a strong financial intermediary not only for the small, poor countries but also for small private sector agents.

The new forms of regional economic cooperation have opened frontiers in the field of development finance. But as trade barriers between member countries fall, the "old wine" of economic infrastructure must be poured into new bottles. Infrastructure bottlenecks must be overcome if the competitiveness of BMCs is to be sustained in world markets. It is a time for optimism and for seizing opportunities. With its reputation as an insider organization with years of solid experience, the Bank is placed to take advantage of, and to reinforce, the outward-looking attitudes now prevalent in the region. The Bank can achieve much to inspire national efforts at development through helping to set priorities at a regional level.

The Bank has traditionally operated in four-year funding cycles. In the future, however, it cannot expect continuously increasing capital increases. The Bank is expected by its members to move from periodic replenishments to a sustainable level of lending following its Eighth Replenishment in 1994. (Sustainable level of lending may be defined as the amount of annual lending that can be committed, in perpetuity, in the absence of fresh replenishments.) The sustainable lending level that the Bank is expected to deliver has been calculated at approximately $7 billion a year. This is based on the Eighth Replenishment's $40 billion capital increase, loan repayments, and additions to reserves.

The Bank may have more time to think and plan for the long term now that it does not need to bargain for funds every four years. Management has new responsibilities to plan strategies and a coherent development philosophy to guide lending. With the new opportunities the Bank must take on a more enterprising role in the context of lending volumes, which are expected to plateau and then decline from the high levels of the early 1990s. Negative resource transfers from the Bank on the part of a good number of BMCs (repayments of principal and interest exceeding new loans) can also be expected, especially from those that will begin to repay the large-scale adjustment loans undertaken in the early 1990s.

The second generation of reforms focusing on social, institutional, budgetary, and public administration issues renews the Bank's difficult staff-intensive role in small-scale operations. The Bank's profitability may decline as a result. This dilemma could result in a delegation of lending activities to smaller, subregional development banks.

Lastly, the painful lesson of the debt crisis of the 1980s was that both the Bank and BMCs were caught unprepared. Just as policy-based lending was introduced to improve project performance, the increasing sensitivity of regional performance to U.S. monetary, fiscal, and exchange rate policies calls for enhanced analytical resources to monitor these policies, to inform BMCs of the expected consequences, and to devise assistance for the successive periods of adjustment. Monitoring of G-7 macroeconomic policies should go hand in hand with country risk analysis. Together they would allow the Bank to be more flexible than under rigid country allocations that are routinely preset for the life of each replenishment. Capital flow predictions have proved elusive; but a sustainable level of lending will require adjusting country programming to changing needs, now dangerously sensitive to international interest rate fluctuations.

The Bank needs to fine-tune its financial assistance, as well as the accompanying policy conditions, to enhance sustainable recovery of the region in the years to come. It must become operationally more flexible and decentralized to meet these new challenges. From the lessons learned from difficult times, the Bank now is better equipped to take advantage of such opportunities.

## Notes

1. On the whole, major borrowers also avoided hard conditionality from the IMF and the World Bank.

2. These are defined as capital inflows less amortizations, interest payments, and dividends.

3. By way of contrast, it should be noted that in the World Bank group, its private lending arm, the International Finance Corporation (IFC), was created ahead of its soft window, the International Development Association (IDA).

4. After the first oil price hike and the oil bonanza in the early 1970s, Venezuela set up a trust fund equivalent to $500 million (including the equivalent of $100 million in bolivars). The terms and conditions of the loans granted with these resources were similar to those governing operations with ordinary capital resources. Special preference was given to joint projects, particularly those that contributed to regional integration. The only other BMC to have established a trust fund, although a much smaller one, was Argentina, which did so in 1970 for financing specific projects in its neighboring countries, Bolivia, Paraguay, and Uruguay.

5. Author's interview with IDB officials.

6. Mexico is a shareholder in the Central American Bank for Economic Integration and sits on the Board as a net donor member. Mexico, Venezuela, and Colombia are also regional, nonborrowing members of the Caribbean Development Bank.

# PART 1

## HISTORICAL SETTING AND RECORD OF PERFORMANCE

# 2

# A Brief History of the Bank

## Institutional Framework

The IDB is the oldest and largest of the regional development banks
(RDBs). It was founded in 1959. Its total subscribed capital reached $64
billion at the end of 1993; its authorized capital was increased by the
Eighth Replenishment in 1994 to $101 billion. The IDB is the chief
development finance agency for Latin America and the Caribbean
region. Its financial and technical resources have supported the regional struggle for social and economic development.

For most, if not all of its BMCs, the Bank has been the largest external source of public capital. At the same time, the BMCs are the majority shareholders. This is an important feature of the Bank: Latin
American governments perceive the IDB as "their" development institution.

Since its founding, the Bank has had three presidents. The first,
Felipe Herrera of Chile, served from 1960 to 1971. He was succeeded
by Antonio Ortiz Mena, who had previously served as Mexico's
finance minister. Ortiz Mena resigned in December 1987 before his
third term was over. Enrique Iglesias, the former secretary general of
the Economic Commission for Latin America and the Caribbean
(ECLAC) and foreign affairs minister of Uruguay, was elected in
February 1988 and took office on April 1, 1988. He has recently been
reelected for a second term. Each president left his imprint on the Bank
and contributed to shaping the economic philosophy and the lending
priorities of the day. Felipe Herrera gave the Bank its credentials and
its image as a catalyst of change. Antonio Ortiz Mena opened the Bank
to new regional and extraregional donor countries and nurtured the
multilateral character of the institution. Enrique Iglesias provided
intellectual leadership and strategic direction.

More than the other RDBs, the IDB has had a close relationship
with the government of the United States. The United States has a larg-

er stake in the IDB than in any other international financial institution: until 1994, it possessed a third of the voting power. This share was reduced to 30 percent at the time of the eighth general resource increase in 1994. Because amendments to the IDB's Articles of Agreement require the consent of two-thirds of regional members the United States, with a three-fourths majority, maintains its veto power over amendments to the Agreement. The United States also controls the timing of capital increases.

The IDB was, until the founding of the European Bank for Reconstruction and Development (EBRD), the only regional bank whose headquarters were not established in a borrowing member country. It has joined the Bretton Woods institutions in the capital of the United States, the country with the largest capital subscription.

### Origins and Mandate

The idea of a regional financial institution was a long-standing one in Latin America, going as far back as the nineteenth century. It gathered force in the mid-1950s when the region's expectations of extensive financial support from the World Bank were disappointed. The Latin American countries had provided nearly one-half of the original membership of the World Bank. But as colonies in other continents gained independence, the field of operations of the World Bank expanded. There was concern that these new members, being at earlier levels of development, would be granted priority for financial assistance. The governments of Latin America made a case for a lending agency that would specialize in the development problems of the region.

In this climate of opinion a special economic conference convened at the end of 1954 in Quitandinha,[1] Brazil, and called for the establishment of a group of experts from central banks and from the Economic Commission for Latin America (ECLA) to make a specific proposal to the Organization of American States (OAS). This group proposed the creation of a development fund to supplement the efforts of existing lending agencies. The idea was rebuffed by the U.S. secretary of the treasury, George Humphrey, on the grounds that the United States did not have the public funds to finance a program of this kind, that any projects in the region could be financed by existing resources, and that, in any case, the foreign resources for financing development should come from the private sector.

The Quitandinha proposals were revived four years later after U.S. vice president Richard Nixon's visit to Latin America contributed to a change of perceptions and priorities. The hostility Nixon encountered on his tour raised awareness in the United States of the deep political, social, and economic unrest in the region and prompted a shift in U.S. policy. Development cooperation was added to its regional agenda over and above military security—a shift that also modified U.S. opposition to proposals of regional integration in Latin America.

The blueprint for the Bank recommended that it fund not only productive projects in the traditional sense but social projects. It proposed to enable the regional bank to finance local projects. It was also envisioned that the Bank should support the process of planning and project preparation by providing technical assistance to define priorities, prepare adequate projects, and inform borrowers about the various steps, conditions, and commitments required (Articles of Agreement, Article I, section 2.v). A distinctive feature of the IDB is its extensive network of field offices. There is a country office in every BMC to channel technical assistance and enhance project supervision.

In addition to mobilizing resources and providing technical assistance, the IDB has an explicit mandate to support regional integration schemes. The Bank's participation in improving the utilization of resources in borrowing members must be "in a manner consistent with the objective of making their economies more complementary" (Article I, section 2.iv). "The purpose of the Bank shall be to contribute to the acceleration of the process of economic development of the member countries, individually and collectively" (ibid). (The Bank, in tandem with regional integration agreements, was an offspring of the prevailing structuralist school of economic thought, which underscored the impact of external bottlenecks in Latin American development.)

Although no preferential financial treatment to projects of regional integration was envisioned, there is a direct relationship between the establishment of the IDB and the early spurt of regional integration in Latin America in the 1960s. A few months after the establishment of the IDB, the Treaty of Montevideo launched the Latin American Free Trade Association (LAFTA) and the Treaty of Managua, the Central American Common Market (CACM). The three institutions were to support integration as a path to industrialization in the region. The Bank was regarded as "the bank for integration." It has granted lines of credit to the Andean Development Corporation and the Central American Bank for Economic Integration and provided technical assistance to several integration schemes.

Nevertheless, integration projects developed and implemented in more than one BMC received no preferential treatment in terms of interest rates, amortization periods, or guarantee requirements. They might qualify for concessional loans, but allocation was not based exclusively on the integration dimension of a project. Only two trust funds established by BMCs, one by Argentina in 1970 and another by Venezuela in 1975, gave priority to the promotion of regional development.

The proclamation by the United States of the Alliance for Progress (which came after the establishment of the IDB) bolstered and nurtured the Bank, defining a role for the Bank in its early years. The alliance placed special emphasis on financing projects of social development with the hope of reducing social tensions and promoting political stability during the height of the Cold War. In 1961 President Kennedy allocated $394 million (later raised to $525 million) to a Social Progress Trust Fund (SPTF) to be administered under a trust agreement by the IDB.

Latin American policymakers, in campaigning for the establishment of the IDB during the 1950s, laid particular emphasis on the need for a regional development bank that would support the private sector in agriculture and industry without government guarantees. They argued that the private sector could be an active development agent if capital were made available. Moreover, a balance had to be drawn between the directly productive sectors and infrastructure; otherwise the development of infrastructure supported by the World Bank could move ahead of the productive capacity to make use of it (Dell 1972).

The Articles of Agreement establishing the IDB requires it "to cooperate with the member countries to orient their development policies toward a better utilization of their resources" (Article I, section 2.a.iv). This aspect of its mandate was interpreted as a responsibility to set up and support planning institutions, to provide assistance in the preparation of projects, to establish or strengthen institutions capable of executing the projects, to train specialists, and to evaluate and improve project implementation. Most of the region's planning offices were organized by a tripartite commission composed of the OAS, the IDB, and ECLA during the early 1960s as part of the Alliance for Progress program. Tripartite cooperation of such magnitude declined after the alliance was shelved, although smaller, joint technical assistance projects remained. More recently, the end of the Cold War and the revival of regionalism have prompted a redefinition of regional institutions; tripartite cooperation may reappear under a new guise.

Until the regional payments crisis in the mid-1980s undermined the foundations of the Bank, it had placed decisionmaking responsibility on the formulation of plans, the definition of policies, and the establishment of priorities with the member countries (C. Morales in Calvo and Tomassini 1970). The IDB was, as described by Sidney Dell, "the servant of the member governments, not their master" (Dell 1972, 233).

The Bank's initial resources were a little less than $1 billion. The first loan was approved in February 1961. It granted $3.9 million for the provision of drinking water and sewerage to the Peruvian city of Arequipa, a project of which Bank officials are still proud today.

Such, in brief, was the intellectual framework in which the Latin American bank and its identity emerged. The IDB was entrusted with two basic tasks: financing investment projects and providing technical assistance. The Bank has reconsidered this mandate at times in light of the changing nature of the problems of the region (and the perceptions of these), the lessons evolving from its operational experience, and the changes in the global economic conditions confronted by borrowers. A major turning point took place during the Seventh Replenishment when the philosophy and operational modalities of the Bank were severely questioned due to repercussions of the debt crisis.

*Membership*

Only members of the Organization of American States were originally eligible for membership. The agreement establishing the IDB was signed by twenty Latin countries (including Cuba, which subsequently did not join) and the United States. In the late 1960s, three newly independent English-speaking Caribbean countries—Trinidad and Tobago, Barbados, and Jamaica—joined. Subsequently, the Bahamas, Surinam, and Guyana also became members. Belize joined in 1992.

The United States was the sole nonborrowing country at the Bank's inception. During the Bank's first decade, the United States held 42.05 percent of the voting power (*Annual Report*, 1970). In 1972 an amendment to the charter allowed the admission of Canada, not then a member of the OAS. The incorporation was opposed by Chile and Peru because of the alteration in the distribution of voting power. Nonregional countries were invited to become members in the mid-1970s. As part of the Fourth Replenishment, a further amendment in 1976 permitted the admission of nonregional "members of the IMF and Switzerland" (Articles of Agreement, Article II). In the course of the following two years, Austria, Belgium, Denmark, Finland, France, Germany, Israel, Italy, Japan, the Netherlands, Spain, Sweden, Switzerland, the United Kingdom, and Yugoslavia[2] became members. Portugal joined in 1980. Norway had applied to join at the same time as the first European countries in the mid-1970s; however, for internal reasons, accession could not be completed until the late 1980s, at which point Brazil tried to obstruct it on the grounds that the "Latin American character of the Bank" needed to be preserved.

The new capital subscriptions that followed the incorporation of the nonregional countries altered the distribution of voting power. The share of BMCs fell from their initial 67.95 percent to 54.8 percent; the U.S. share fell from 42.05 percent to 34.5 percent (see Table 2.1). The

Table 2.1    Evolution of Voting Power Groups

|  | 1980<br>% of Votes | 1994<br>% of Votes |
|---|---|---|
| Regional BMCs |  |  |
| Group A |  |  |
| Argentina | 11.88 | 10.75 |
| Brazil | 11.88 | 10.75 |
| Mexico | 7.64 | 6.91 |
| Venezuela | 6.37 | 5.76 |
| Subtotal | 37.77 | 34.17 |
| Group B |  |  |
| Chile | 3.27 | 2.95 |
| Colombia | 3.27 | 2.95 |
| Peru | 1.60 | 1.44 |
| Subtotal | 8.14 | 7.34 |
| Group C |  |  |
| Bahamas | 0.19 | 0.21 |
| Barbados | 0.15 | 0.13 |
| Costa Rica | 0.49 | 0.43 |
| Jamaica | 0.65 | 0.57 |
| Trinidad and Tobago | 0.49 | 0.43 |
| Uruguay | 1.28 | 1.15 |
| Subtotal | 3.25 | 2.92 |
| Group D |  |  |
| Belize | — | 0.11 |
| Bolivia | 0.96 | 0.86 |
| Dominican Republic | 0.65 | 0.57 |
| El Salvador | — | 0.43 |
| Ecuador | 0.65 | 0.57 |
| Guatemala | 0.65 | 0.57 |
| Guyana | 0.19 | 0.16 |
| Haiti | 0.49 | 0.43 |
| Honduras | 0.49 | 0.43 |
| Nicaragua | 0.49 | 0.43 |
| Panama | 0.49 | 0.43 |
| Paraguay | 0.49 | 0.43 |
| Surinam | 0.11 | 0.09 |
| Subtotal | 5.66 | 5.51 |
| Total BMCs | 54.82 | 49.94 |
| Regional nonborrowing members |  |  |
| United States | 34.55 | 30.00 |
| Canada | 4.56 | 4.00 |
| Subtotal | 39.11 | 34.00 |
| Nonregional, nonborrowing members |  |  |
| Austria | 0.06 | 0.16 |
| Belgium | 0.17 | 0.33 |
| Croatia | — | 0.05 |
| Denmark | 0.08 | 0.17 |
| Finland | 0.06 | 0.16 |
| France | 0.66 | 1.89 |
| Germany | 0.85 | 1.89 |

*(continues)*

Table 2.1    continued

| | 1980<br>% of Votes | 1994<br>% of Votes |
|---|---|---|
| Nonregional, nonborrowing members (continued) | | |
| Israel | 0.06 | 0.15 |
| Italy | 0.66 | 1.89 |
| Japan | 0.92 | 5.00 |
| Netherlands | 0.07 | 0.34 |
| Norway | — | 0.17 |
| Portugal | 0.02 | 0.05 |
| Slovenia | — | 0.03 |
| Spain | 0.78 | 1.89 |
| Sweden | 0.19 | 0.32 |
| Switzerland | 0.10 | 0.47 |
| United Kingdom | 0.83 | 0.96 |
| Bosnia/Yugoslavia | — | 0.03 |
| Subtotal | 5.51 | 15.95 |
| Total | 100.00 | 100.00 |

*Source:* IDB, *Annual Reports*, various years.

nonregional members held a 7.09 percent stake[3] and were given two seats on the Board. To accommodate the entry of nonregional, nonborrowing members, the Inter-Regional Capital Account was created. It operated under the same guidelines as those applied to ordinary capital except that subscriptions were from nonregional, nonborrowing members. In 1988 both accounts were merged, and they are now a single ordinary capital account. Today the Bank has forty-six members.

After the accession of Canada and the nonregional, nonborrowing members in the mid-1970s, the number of Board members stood at eleven. In 1978 the Board was reorganized, and a new constituency was added to give the English-speaking Caribbean countries a seat of their own. Four chairs represented the nonborrowing members, of which two belonged to the nonregional countries, one to Canada and one to the United States. Since split voting is not allowed, each constituency must compromise to put forth a single vote (see Table 2.2).

A new change in the capital structure of the Bank was decided during the Eighth Replenishment, more than doubling the stake of the nonregional, nonborrowing members from 7.09 percent to 15.95 percent. Two new seats were added to the Board, one for Japan, which has increased its stake from 1.07 percent to 5 percent, and the other for Chile (to be shared with other BMCs). Chile had been the only one of the five biggest BMCs that did not have a seat on the Board. When the Bank was first created, Chile gave up its chair in exchange for the presidency of the Bank. When Felipe Herrera was succeeded by Ortiz Mena from Mexico, Chile, then governed by the Unidad Popular administration of Salvador Allende, discovered that its entitlements in

**Table 2.2   Composition of the Board of Executive Directors**

| Country of Executive Director and Alternate (A) | Appointed or Elected by | Percentage of Votes |
|---|---|---|
| **1970** | | |
| Argentina | Argentina | 12.42 |
| Peru (A) | Peru | 1.70 |
| Subtotal | | 14.12 |
| Brazil | Brazil | 12.42 |
| Ecuador (A) | Ecuador | 0.71 |
| Subtotal | | 13.13 |
| Honduras | Costa Rica | 0.55 |
| Nicaragua (A) | El Salvador | 0.55 |
| | Guatemala | 0.71 |
| | Haiti | 0.55 |
| | Honduras | 0.55 |
| | Nicaragua | 0.55 |
| Subtotal | | 3.46 |
| Mexico | Barbados | 0.19 |
| Panama (A) | Dominican Republic | 0.71 |
| | Jamaica | 0.71 |
| | Mexico | 8.00 |
| | Panama | 0.55 |
| Subtotal | | 10.16 |
| Paraguay | Bolivia | 1.04 |
| Bolivia (A) | Paraguay | 0.55 |
| | Uruguay | 1.37 |
| Subtotal | | 2.96 |
| Venezuela | Chile | 3.45 |
| Colombia (A) | Colombia | 3.44 |
| | Trinidad and Tobago | 0.55 |
| | Venezuela | 6.66 |
| Subtotal | | 14.10 |
| United States | United States | 42.05 |
| United States (A) | United States | |
| Total | | 100.00 |
| **1980** | | |
| Argentina | Argentina | 11.88 |
| Chile (A) | Chile | 3.27 |
| Subtotal | | 15.15 |
| Brazil | Brazil | 11.88 |
| Ecuador (A) | Ecuador | 0.65 |
| Subtotal | | 12.53 |
| Costa Rica | Costa Rica | 0.49 |
| El Salvador (A) | El Salvador | 0.49 |
| | Guatemala | 0.65 |
| | Haiti | 0.49 |
| | Honduras | 0.49 |
| | Nicaragua | 0.49 |
| Subtotal | | 3.10 |
| Mexico | Mexico | 7.64 |
| Dominican Republic (A) | Dominican Republic | 0.65 |
| Subtotal | | 8.29 |
| Paraguay | Paraguay | 0.49 |
| Bolivia (A) | Bolivia | 0.96 |
| | Uruguay | 1.28 |
| Subtotal | | 2.73 |

*(continues)*

**Table 2.2    continued**

| Country of Executive Director and Alternate (A) | Appointed or Elected by | Percentage of Votes |
|---|---|---|
| 1980 (continued) | | |
| Venezuela | Venezuela | 6.37 |
| Panama (A) | Panama | 0.49 |
| Subtotal | | 6.86 |
| Colombia | Columbia | 3.27 |
| Peru (A) | Peru | 1.60 |
| Subtotal | | 4.87 |
| Barbados | Barbados | 0.15 |
| Jamaica (A) | Jamaica | 0.65 |
| | Guyana | 0.19 |
| | Trinidad and Tobago | 0.49 |
| | Bahamas | 0.19 |
| Subtotal | | 1.67 |
| United States | United States | 34.55 |
| United States (A) | United States | |
| Canada | Canada | 4.56 |
| Canada (A) | Canada | |
| Spain | Austria | 0.06 |
| Switzerland (A) | France | 0.66 |
| | Israel | 0.06 |
| | Japan | 0.92 |
| | Portugal | 0.06 |
| | Spain | 0.78 |
| | Switzerland | 0.19 |
| | Yugoslavia | 0.06 |
| Subtotal | | 2.79 |
| United Kingdom | Germany | 0.85 |
| Netherlands (A) | Belgium | 0.17 |
| | Denmark | 0.08 |
| | Finland | 0.06 |
| | Italy | 0.66 |
| | Netherlands | 0.07 |
| | United Kingdom | 0.83 |
| | Sweden | 0.19 |
| Subtotal | | 2.91 |
| Total | | 100.00 |

| Country of Executive Director | Appointed or Elected by | Percentage of Votes |
|---|---|---|
| 1994 Regional Constituencies | | |
| Argentina | Argentina | 10.75 |
| | Haiti | 0.43 |
| Subtotal | | 11.18 |
| Brazil | Brazil | 10.75 |
| | Surinam | 0.09 |
| Subtotal | | 10.84 |
| Uruguay | Uruguay | 1.15 |
| Paraguay | Paraguay | 0.43 |
| Bolivia | Bolivia | 0.86 |
| Subtotal | | 2.44 |
| Colombia | Colombia | 2.95 |
| Chile | Chile | 2.95 |
| Peru | Peru | 1.44 |
| | Ecuador | 0.57 |
| Subtotal | | 7.91 |

(continues)

**Table 2.2    continued**

| Country of Executive Director | Appointed or Elected by | Percentage of Votes |
|---|---|---|
| **1994** | | |
| **Regional Constituencies (continued)** | | |
| Mexico | Mexico | 6.91 |
| | Dominican Republic | 0.57 |
| Subtotal | | 7.48 |
| Venezuela | Venezuela | 5.76 |
| | Panama | 0.43 |
| Subtotal | | 6.19 |
| Costa Rica | Costa Rica | 0.43 |
| El Salvador | El Salvador | 0.43 |
| Guatemala | Guatemala | 0.57 |
| Honduras | Honduras | 0.43 |
| Nicaragua | Nicaragua | 0.43 |
| Belize | Belize | 0.11 |
| Subtotal | | 2.40 |
| Bahamas | Bahamas | 0.21 |
| Barbados | Barbados | 0.13 |
| Guyana | Guyana | 0.16 |
| Jamaica | Jamaica | 0.57 |
| Trinidad and Tobago | Trinidad and Tobago | 0.43 |
| Subtotal | | 1.50 |
| United States | United States | 30.00 |
| Canada | Canada | 4.00 |
| Total | | 83.94 |
| **1994** | | |
| **Nonregional Constituencies** | | |
| Japan | Japan | 5.00 |
| | United Kingdom | 0.93 |
| | Portugal | 0.05 |
| | Croatia | 0.05 |
| | Slovenia | 0.03 |
| Subtotal | | 6.06 |
| France | France | 1.89 |
| Spain | Spain | 1.89 |
| | Sweden | 0.33 |
| | Norway | 0.17 |
| | Denmark | 0.17 |
| | Finland | 0.16 |
| | Austria | 0.16 |
| Subtotal | | 4.77 |
| Germany | Germany | 1.89 |
| Italy | Italy | 1.89 |
| | Belgium | 0.33 |
| | Netherlands | 0.34 |
| | Switzerland | 0.47 |
| | Israel | 0.16 |
| Subtotal | | 5.08 |
| Total | | 15.91 |

*Source:* IDB, *Annual Reports,* various years.

*Note:* Countries are grouped by constituencies. Countries in the first column take the chair of their group by rotation. The Colombia, Chile, Peru group has two seats. Within groups as shown, the chair rotates. Alternates are not shown in this table.

Figures are rounded to two decimal points.

international organizations were diminished. In the late 1970s, when the Argentine and Chilean military developed cooperative ties, Argentina offered to share the seat but not on a rotating basis. Thus, until the Eighth Replenishment, Chile had only an alternate executive director (see Table 2.3).

The ratio between the regional and nonregional members for capital shares and voting power now stands at 83 to 16 percent (and between nonborrowers and borrowers at fifty-fifty). The structure of governance still remains heavily influenced by the major donor and the four largest BMCs, which together hold two-thirds of the voting power.

The U.S. stake in the Bank is higher than in any other multilateral development bank. Informally too, the United States has a strong influence due not only to the location of headquarters but also to the fact that the executive vice president, who is the chief administrator of the Bank, has always been a U.S. citizen. The financial manager and the general counsel have also traditionally been U.S. nationals. About a quarter of top management today are U.S. citizens. This share has declined from over 40 percent in the early 1970s (U.S. Congress 1974).[4]

As suggested by John White before the accession of the nonregional countries and Canada, the IDB has followed "a pattern shaped by two interacting sets of relationships—the Latin American countries' relationships with each other, and their collective and individual relationships with the U.S.A." (White 1970, 140). The pattern did not change much after the new nonborrowing countries were incorporated. The United States remained the single most important contributor and thus the most involved of all external institutions in screening loans and in making its economic preferences known. But the pattern has followed some pendulum swings. In the mid-1970s when there arose disputes over the nationalization of U.S. firms in Chile and Peru and U.S. power was perceived as excessive, these countries, with the support of Argentina, suggested moving the IDB headquarters from Washington to Latin America (IDB, *Proceedings*, 1972). Two decades later, the waning of Cold War antagonisms allowed a more collaborative atmosphere. Coupled with the widespread acceptance of market-based open economies and the promises of the Enterprise for the Americas Initiative, the position of the United States as a leading contributor is at present more accepted by Latin American policymakers. The initiative was little more than a set of vague promises, but it struck an enthusiastic chord in the hearts and minds of most Latin American leaders and officials. Latin American relations with the United States are now smoother than they have been for years. But, as a reflection of the changing distribution of global economic power, U.S. hegemony is being increasingly contested by other nonborrowing countries.

**Table 2.3    Subscriptions to Capital Stock and Voting Power at End of IDB-8**

| Regional Borrowing Countries | Total Shares | Total Amount ($ Millions) | Percent Voting Power |
|---|---|---|---|
| Group A | | | |
| Argentina | 900,154 | 10,858.95 | 10.749 |
| Brazil | 900,154 | 10,858.95 | 10.749 |
| Mexico | 578,632 | 6,980.29 | 6.910 |
| Venezuela | 482,267 | 5,817.80 | 5.760 |
| Subtotal | 2,861,207 | 34,515.99 | 34.168 |
| Group B | | | |
| Chile | 247,074 | 2,980.56 | 2.952 |
| Colombia | 247,074 | 2,980.56 | 2.952 |
| Peru | 120,622 | 1,455.12 | 1.442 |
| Subtotal | 614,770 | 7,416.24 | 7.346 |
| Group C | | | |
| Bahamas | 17,398 | 209.88 | 0.209 |
| Barbados | 10,767 | 129.89 | 0.130 |
| Costa Rica | 36,121 | 435.74 | 0.433 |
| Trinidad and Tobago | 36,121 | 435.74 | 0.433 |
| Uruguay | 96,507 | 1,164.21 | 1.154 |
| Subtotal | 196,914 | 2,375.46 | 2.359 |
| Group D | | | |
| Belize | 9,178 | 110.72 | 0.111 |
| Bolivia | 72,258 | 871.68 | 0.864 |
| Dominican Republic | 48,220 | 581.70 | 0.577 |
| Ecuador | 48,220 | 581.70 | 0.577 |
| El Salvador | 36,121 | 435.74 | 0.433 |
| Guatemala | 48,220 | 581.70 | 0.577 |
| Guyana | 13,393 | 161.57 | 0.162 |
| Haiti | 36,121 | 435.74 | 0.433 |
| Honduras | 36,121 | 435.74 | 0.433 |
| Nicaragua | 36,121 | 435.74 | 0.433 |
| Panama | 36,121 | 435.74 | 0.433 |
| Paraguay | 36,121 | 435.74 | 0.433 |
| Surinam | 7,342 | 88.57 | 0.089 |
| Subtotal | 463,557 | 5,592.08 | 5.555 |
| Total | 4,136,448 | 49,899.77 | 49.428 |

| Regional Nonborrowing Countries | Total Shares | Total Amount ($ Millions) | Percent Voting Power |
|---|---|---|---|
| Canada | 334,887 | 4,039.89 | 4.000 |
| United States | 2,512,529 | 30,309.72 | 30.000 |
| Total | 2,847,416 | 34,349.61 | 34.000 |

| Nonregional countries | Total Shares | Total Amount ($ Millions) | Percent Voting Power |
|---|---|---|---|
| Japan | 418,642 | 5,050.26 | 5.000 |
| Austria | 13,312 | 160.59 | 0.161 |
| Belgium | 27,438 | 331.00 | 0.329 |
| Croatia | 4,018 | 48.47 | 0.050 |
| Denmark | 14,157 | 170.78 | 0.171 |
| Finland | 13,312 | 160.59 | 0.161 |
| France | 158,637 | 1,913.71 | 1.896 |
| Germany | 158,641 | 1,913.75 | 1.896 |
| Israel | 13,126 | 158.34 | 0.158 |
| Italy | 158,637 | 1,913.71 | 1.896 |

*(continues)*

**Table 2.3    continued**

| Nonregional countries (continued) | Total Shares | Total Amount ($ Millions) | Percent Voting Power |
|---|---|---|---|
| Netherlands | 28,207 | 340.27 | 0.338 |
| Norway | 14,157 | 170.78 | 0.171 |
| Portugal | 4,474 | 53.97 | 0.055 |
| Slovenia | 2,434 | 29.36 | 0.031 |
| Spain | 158,637 | 1,913.71 | 1.896 |
| Sweden | 27,268 | 328.95 | 0.327 |
| Switzerland | 39,347 | 474.66 | 0.471 |
| United Kingdom | 80,551 | 971.72 | 0.963 |
| Bosnia/Yugoslavia | 1,984 | 23.93 | 0.027 |
| Subtotal | 1,336,979 | 16,128.59 | 15.997 |
| Total | 8,320,843 | 100,377.97 | 99.425 |

*Source:* IDB.
*Note:* Of the total shareholdings, 4.3 percent is paid-in capital, and the remainder is callable.

## Voting Procedures

The resources provided by the member countries to finance the Bank's operations are structured into two separate windows, the ordinary capital resources and the Fund for Special Operations. Voting procedures differ for each. The Seventh Replenishment marked a turning point for loan approvals from the ordinary capital account. It was approved in 1989 after an acrimonious three-year negotiation that got stuck on those same voting procedures. Until that point decisions by the Board on ordinary lending operations were subject to a simple majority rule, so that no single country had veto power. All decisions concerning concessional loans from the FSO, however, have required a two-thirds majority (Article IV, section 9), so that from its inception veto power lay with the United States—as well as, theoretically, with combinations of borrowers. The reason for this difference between the hard and the soft windows is that the United States contributed less than one-half of the subscribed capital of the Bank, but it provided more than two-thirds of the resources for the FSO while the remaining third was paid in by the developing countries in Groups A and B.[5]

When the nonregional countries joined the Bank at the Sixth Replenishment in the course of 1976 and 1977, they were asked (as a form of entry fee) to contribute a larger share of the burden of concessional resources than the voting power they were granted. The U.S. contribution to the FSO declined to about 40 percent, but the two-thirds majority rule was not changed. The relative burden sharing in FSO vis-à-vis voting share is evidenced in Table 2.4 below. At the Eighth Replenishment in early 1994, funds for the FSO were raised mainly with contributions from the nonregional, nonborrowing members, who provided 80 percent of the new funds.

Table 2.4    Voting Share in Relation to FSO Contributions

|  | GRI-6 | | | GRI-8 | | |
|---|---|---|---|---|---|---|
|  | 1 | 2 | 3 | 1 | 2 | 3 |
| United States | 34.61 | 41.27 | 1.2 | 30.02 | 8.22 | 0.3 |
| Nonregionals | 7.17 | 25.33 | 3.5 | 15.98 | 80.00 | 5.0 |
| Canada | 4.38 | 5.56 | 1.3 | 4.00 | 2.00 | 0.5 |
| BMCs | 53.84 | 27.84 | 0.5 | 50.00 | 10.50 | 0.2 |

*Source:* Derived from IDB annual reports.
*Key:* (1) voting share (percent); (2) FSO share (percent); (3) ratio of FSO share/voting share

The organization has suffered from mistrust between Board and management and between recipients and nonborrowers. This management view and style produced an organization with little delegation (IDB, *Revised Report*, 1989). The Board of Executive Directors has been actively involved in the day-to-day administrative issues and has scrutinized loans closely before approval. Such micromanagement has led to a heavy workload that has diverted the Board's time and efforts from substantial policy issues. The Board's hands-on role was heavily criticized by the 1993 task force convened to assess portfolio management (IDB, *Managing for Effective Development,* 1993).

The Committee of the Whole of the Board undertakes active consultations with the staff and with member governments and conducts an intensive oral review of each loan document.[6] Until the 1988 reorganization of the Bank, questions were raised with the manager of the operations department. Since then the process of consultation is conducted with the project team. The committee may, on the basis of the review, call for changes in the operation. This prerogative, however, has rarely been used. If an executive director requires clarification, it is usually sought outside formal Board meetings; loan proposals have not been referred to management for design reasons.

The IDB has had conflicts over lending operations, but they have usually been settled before formal voting took place. In theory, the BMCs, by voting together, could approve an operation without the consent of the nonborrowing members. In practice, this has not occurred. The Board has operated on the basis of consensus, and loans over which there is controversy have been postponed until agreement is reached. There have been instances when loan proposals were withdrawn before reaching voting stage after informal consultations with the administration and members of the Board indicated that the necessary support would not be forthcoming. In such cases, the voting procedures of the Bank are a safeguard for the major nonborrower, rather than the primary means whereby it secures acceptance of its point of view.

Borrowing member countries have shown self-control and self-censorship; there is no record of any loan having been approved through reliance solely on the Latin American majority. This is not to say that loans put before the Board always had prior consent from the United States. Nonborrowing countries were not always in full agreement. Thus a loan that was not expected to be approved by the United States might nevertheless be put before the Board if other nonborrowing member countries could be counted upon to counterbalance U.S. opposition.

A U.S. Government Accounting Office (GAO) report to the Congress in 1972 noted that "in seeking to avoid open confrontations with the Latin American members, U.S. officials should work quietly behind the scenes to keep IDB management from submitting loan proposals to the Board of Executive Directors for approval, and in this manner, delay loan proposals for several months" (quoted by Sovani 1980, 78). In short, the Latin American majority was never used, and some BMCs felt resentment because management avoided the submission of loans that did not have prior U.S. approval, making bilateral negotiations with the United States necessary.

Inevitably, as the chief source of funds, the United States was in a position to have its views prevail over a specific issue, even without the need to resort to veto power. The BMCs have been well aware of the vital importance of enlisting resources from the United States and of the importance of U.S. support to the Bank's creditworthiness; they have thus tended to accept U.S. inclinations without tinkering with percentages. They have consistently avoided forcing operations through the Board so that open confrontation has seldom, if ever, occurred.[7]

Nonetheless, in the course of negotiations for the Seventh Replenishment (1985–1989) the United States maintained that the Bank was unresponsive to U.S. concerns and priorities. The United States was willing to support a substantial capital increase if it could obtain agreement on a reform of the Articles of Agreement to change the voting structure and acquire an effective veto over operations. Without such reform it was unprepared to support a substantial capital increase. The position became known as the "big bank–small bank" strategy. Reform of the articles was resisted by BMCs both on political and on practical grounds. One obstacle was that newly established congresses in nascent, Latin American democracies could no longer govern by decree. The compromise after four years of negotiations, which almost brought the Bank to a standstill, was found in a parallel voting mechanism that left the articles intact.

The new loan approval procedure provided nonborrowing members with greater safeguards over lending operations than could be derived from their formal voting power. Members became entitled to delay loan approvals if they objected to proposals submitted to the Board. A single director obtained the right to delay a loan for an initial period of two months; after that period any two directors had the right to delay for a five-month period. After that time three directors with 40 percent of the votes could delay the loan proposal for another five months. After a seven-month delay the president could intervene to resubmit the loan to the Board. To obtain 40 percent of the votes the major shareholder, the United States, would need support from at least two other nonborrowing chairs (in other words, Canada and one nonregional or two nonregional chairs). The practical implication of this was an overall shift in influence in favor of all non-BMCs. Canada and the nonregional members also increased their potential influence and might provide a balancing role. During the Eighth Replenishment, against the backdrop of the new spirit of regional collaboration, the delay periods have been shortened. One director can delay ordinary capital loans in the Committee of the Whole for one month, and thereafter two or more directors have a right to only two additional months.

The loan-delaying powers have so far been exercised only once in a controversial fashion. In early 1991 the four directors representing the G-7 countries agreed to suspend agreement over a $300 million sewerage loan to Brazil. The question was not the quality of the loan but concern over mounting arrears on Brazil's private debt. The move did not muster unqualified support from all nonborrowing countries. Both nonregional chairs, despite voting in favor of the delay, made a statement that the non-G-7 countries in their respective constituencies were not in agreement. The loan was cleared some months later when Brazil agreed to settle its $8 billion interest backlog with commercial banks.

## The Inter-American Investment Corporation

The Inter-American Investment Corporation (IIC) started operations in 1989. While affiliated with the IDB, it functions as a separate entity with autonomous management. The chairman of the Board is the president of the Bank, but the Bank is not a shareholder of the corporation (see Table 2.5).

The IIC's mission is to finance private sector investment projects without government guarantees. It complements the Bank's priority for small and medium-sized companies. The IIC's initial subscribed capital stock was $200 million, and it began with a $210 million loan from the Bank. In addition, the Corporation raises funds from the

Table 2.5    Inter-American Investment Corporation Capital Structure

| Members | Shareholding % |
| --- | --- |
| Argentina | 11.6 |
| Austria | 0.5 |
| Bahamas | 0.2 |
| Barbados | 0.1 |
| Bolivia | 0.9 |
| Brazil | 11.6 |
| Chile | 3.4 |
| Colombia | 3.4 |
| Costa Rica | 0.4 |
| Dominican Republic | 0.6 |
| Ecuador | 0.6 |
| El Salvador | 0.4 |
| France | 3.1 |
| Germany | 3.1 |
| Guatemala | 0.6 |
| Guyana | 0.1 |
| Haiti | 0.4 |
| Honduras | 0.4 |
| Israel | 0.2 |
| Italy | 3.1 |
| Jamaica | 0.6 |
| Japan | 3.1 |
| Mexico | 7.4 |
| Netherlands | 1.5 |
| Nicaragua | 0.4 |
| Panama | 0.4 |
| Paraguay | 0.4 |
| Peru | 2.1 |
| Spain | 3.1 |
| Switzerland | 1.5 |
| Trinidad and Tobago | 0.4 |
| Uruguay | 1.2 |
| United States | 25.5 |
| Venezuela | 6.2 |
| Total | 98.5 |

Source: IIC Eighth Annual Report 1993.
Note: As of December 31, 1993.

markets, though its borrowing capacity has been limited by the tight debt-to-equity guidelines set out in its charter.

IIC operations take the form of loans, equity investment, or guarantees. It can invest in new companies or the expansion, modernization, restructuring, or privatization of existing ones. It has a limit of $10 million per operation. The large majority of loans range between $2 million and $6 million. The IIC has mobilized funds directly and indirectly. By mid-1993 the IIC approved loans for $374 million; the total cost of funded projects amounted to $1.7 billion. In other words, for every dollar invested by the IIC, $4 was provided by other sources. At that point nearly all its initial resources had been committed, and shareholders have been debating ways in which to strengthen its finances, including:

- a capital increase
- a commitment from the Bank of a portion of its net income
- direct capitalization by the IDB as a shareholder
- an increase in borrowing capacity

Discussions on these matters have been stalemated due to lack of U.S. enthusiasm for the IIC and unwillingness on the part of European and Latin members to inject new capital or lending capacity without the participation of the United States.

## Notes

1. The groundwork for Quitandinha was laid by a group of experts among whom were Eduardo Frei Montalva (chairman), who later became president of Chile, and Carlos Lleras Restrepo (rapporteur), later president of Colombia.

2. Bank membership changed in 1993 when Yugoslavia ceased to be a member and Croatia and Slovenia became members by succession (IDB, *Annual Report*, 1993).

3. Amendments to the Agreement require a two-thirds majority of governors representing three-fourths of the total voting power of the member countries. Unanimity, however, is required for the approval of any amendment modifying the right to withdraw from the Bank, to purchase capital stock of the Bank, and to contribute to the soft loan window, the Fund for Special Operations.

4. There are additional informal agreements under which senior management positions are reserved for specific countries.

5. See Table 2.1 for grouping of member countries. Groups A and B are the more-developed borrowing members; Group C the middle-sized, and Group D the least-developed countries.

6. In this respect the procedure differs from that of the World Bank where executive directors generally accept the loan document as presented by management.

7. For example, see Dell 1972, 41, for a discussion about the currency repayments into the FSO at the Third Replenishment, 1971–1973.

# 3

## Evolution of the Lending Program

The IDB has actively generated resources for its BMCs since it began operation. Lending policies and access to resources are adjusted from time to time to match changing needs with the availability of funds. The distribution of resources among countries and sectors has been negotiated at the time of each replenishment. The Eighth Replenishment freed the Bank from returning to the shareholders every four years. In essence this entailed greater responsibilities placed on management to impose a strategic direction on the lending program, to design appropriate country programs, and to safeguard the Bank's portfolio.

The first two sections of this chapter analyze the IDB's operational policies and the structure of its resources and lending facilities. The third section describes the pattern of loan allocation among countries and suggests the changes that should be made in the future. The fourth section outlines the changes in the sectoral division of labor between the IDB and the World Bank over the decades. Finally, there is an account of the institutional renewal that led to the introduction of policy-based lending and the restoration of the Bank's presence in the region after the economic collapse of the 1980s.

### Basic Operational Policies

During its first three decades, the IDB concentrated on project lending. The agreement establishing the IDB limited it to financing "principally" specific projects. As is well known, nonproject lending has been less typical of multilateral than bilateral channels where it makes up a high proportion of assistance. The main advantage of the project

35

approach (over general support for a program or balance-of-payments plans) is that it could be ascertained that the funds were being used efficiently and for the intended purposes.[1] Yet the agreement also stipulates that "the Bank may make or guarantee over-all loans to development institutions or similar agencies of the members in order that the latter may facilitate the financing of specific development projects whose individual financing requirements are not, in the opinion of the Bank, large enough to warrant the direct supervision of the Bank" (Article III, section 7.a.vi).

Thus project lending in the IDB, as in the World Bank, has encompassed not only physical construction but wholesaling of funds with so-called global loans, which involve an intermediary development financing institution (DFI) that in turn lends the resources to local applicants, individuals, or firms. Usually the ultimate recipients have been small and medium-sized firms. Such global loans have allowed the IDB to support the private sector priorities of BMCs and to allow small firms easy access to credit. About one-third of the loans made to agriculture, industry, and mining have been channeled through DFIs.[2]

The Bank modifies and refines its operating policies as it gains experience and the needs of its BMCs change. Over the years, some DFIs received excessive subsidization; others became insolvent. Traditional global loans are being gradually replaced by less dirigiste methods with on-lending and credit auctioning through the commercial banking system.[3] In 1992 such loans amounted to only 11 percent of lending (IDB, *The Inter-American Development Bank Group*, 1993). This share needs to be increased if the Bank expects to compensate for the fragmented local capital markets confronted by BMCs and spread access to credit to small and medium-sized firms.

The Bank first became involved in program lending in the 1970s. Since that time its approach has undergone some changes. In late 1979, following the Fifth Replenishment and a mandate to benefit low-income people, the Bank began financing sectoral programs with special priority given to agricultural and rural development. A sectoral program loan was used to finance related activities in a development program. This "umbrella" loan combined projects, agencies, and activities of a more variegated nature than in specific project loans. It could cover, for example, the provision of agricultural services, the purchase of seeds and capital equipment, technical cooperation, assistance with marketing of produce, provision of rural schools, and so on. Its broad-based nature made it possible to assist low-income population groups that were otherwise out of the reach of specific projects or global loans for the private sector.

As the region's priorities changed from economic development to financial survival, these early sectoral development operations were abandoned in favor of sectoral adjustment loans. At the Seventh Replenishment, adjustment lending was introduced[4] to provide BMCs with balance-of-payments support and to help them reform distorted sectoral policies that inhibited growth and reduced the impact of projects. Adjustment operations at the IDB have been applied only to sectors and have excluded the broader structural adjustment loans (SALs) offered at the World Bank. The broad objective of adjustment lending was to improve the efficiency and competitiveness of economies facing severe external and internal disequilibria. By being "fast disbursing," this loan type induced policy reforms and eased the short-term costs of adjustment.

As a safeguard mechanism, the United States asked that, for the first two years, adjustment lending be undertaken in coordination with the World Bank, which would act as a custodian of the overall adjustment framework. This liaison would allow IDB staff to be trained in such operations. Thus, coordination and cooperation with the World Bank was strengthened, and the staff of both banks worked closer together. Cross participation or joint missions were developed, and program negotiations were closely coordinated. Analyses and models have been regularly shared by the staffs of the institutions in each operation. Once IDB staff learned to do independent policy analysis, the requirement to work under the World Bank umbrella was withdrawn. Since 1992 the IDB has gradually undertaken adjustment operations on its own and has displayed the capacity to take the lead in policy discussions.[5]

## Resources

The IDB has operated in four-year funding cycles. The necessary capital increase, as well as the guidelines for the lending program to which it will be applied, are negotiated jointly by the Board of Governors, the highest governing body of the Bank. During replenishment negotiations the policies and practices of the Bank are scrutinized. The First and Second Replenishments were relatively easy and increased the callable capital without any corresponding increase in the paid-in portion, which, when first established in 1960, represented 47 percent of total capital resources. The Third Replenishment entailed the first increase in paid-in as well as callable capital; it was agreed upon in 1970 (IDB, *Proposal for an Increase*, 1970). Since then the share of paid-in capital has continuously declined, reaching 2.5 percent at the Eighth Replenishment (see Table 3.1).

Table 3.1    Replenishments: Main Goals and Policy Initiatives

| Replenishment | | GCI | FSO | Main Policy Initiatives |
|---|---|---|---|---|
| III: | 1971–1974 | $2bn | $1.5m | • First increase in paid-in as well as callable capital;<br>• FSO lending restricted to Groups C and D, and repayment in local currencies ceased. |
| IV: | 1975–1978 | $3.9bn | $1m | • Contributions to FSO to be made in convertible currencies;<br>• amendment to incorporate nonregional donors. |
| V: | 1979–1982 | $8bn | $1.5m | • Introduction of the low-income goal;<br>• indicative targets for rural and urban development;<br>• energy and support to external sector. |
| VI: | 1983–1986 | $15bn | $703m | • Creation of the Intermediary Financing Facility for Groups C and D;<br>• retention of indicative targets of the Fifth Replenishment. |
| VII: | 1990–1993 | $26.5bn | $200m | • Introduction of policy-based lending up to a maximum of 25 percent of total and country programming;<br>• introduction of "parallel voting mechanism";<br>• special financial incentives for social projects in the matrix. |
| VIII: | 1994 | $40bn | $1,000m | • Introduction of the sustainable level of lending concept;<br>• new facility for private sector loans without government guarantees;<br>• 40 percent of total lending and 50 percent of the number of operations to be delivered to social needs, equity, and poverty reduction;<br>• introduction of an information disclosure policy and an independent panel to investigate allegations of affected parties;<br>• focus on environmental management and sustainability;<br>• reform of the capital structure to allow greater participation from nonregional donors;<br>• creation of seat on the Board for Japan. |

*Source:* Author's elaboration from replenishment documents.

The backbone of the Bank's resources consists of its ordinary capital and its soft window, the FSO. Ordinary capital resources consist mainly of funds borrowed in capital markets (with the backing of its callable capital), capital paid in by member countries, retained earnings, and loan repayments. Contributions are in proportion to shareholdings, which are negotiated during replenishments.[6] From 1964 these resources were increased by means of eight replenishments.

According to the provisions of the agreement, these resources were to be used for operations that were repayable in the currency or currencies in which the loan was made.

The FSO depends exclusively on government contributions except for some income derived from liquid investments and interest payments. According to Article IV of the agreement it can make loans "on terms and conditions appropriate for dealing with special circumstances arising in specific countries or with respect to specific projects." This facility attracted BMCs to borrow abroad and undertake projects that until then had been considered beyond the scope of international financing. It has also been replenished every four years, although not at the same accelerated pace as ordinary capital resources because donors were suffering aid fatigue and because there were competing demands for aid in other parts of the developing world. At the Seventh Replenishment at the height of the debt crisis, concessional funds reached their lowest point (in relative terms equivalent to less than one percent of the capital increase).

Aid fatigue, however, did not stop replenishments to the soft windows of other MDBs; the World Bank's International Development Association, the Asian Development Fund, and the African Development Fund continued to increase. Donors contended that the Latin American and Caribbean region contained only two of the world's poorest countries, Bolivia and Haiti. Therefore, they allocated a lower priority for assistance to this region. This logic is contestable if one looks at the number of poor in the region rather than average per capita GNP. One hundred and eighty million people, or two out of five persons in Latin America, live in poverty today. One half of these endure abject poverty, with incomes too low to purchase a minimally adequate diet. Some of the larger countries, the most striking case being Brazil, have massive poverty problems, featuring a very unequal income distribution but a relatively high income per capita.[7]

The terms of the contributions to the soft window have varied. Initially all contributions to FSO resources, including those from Latin American countries, were made in national currencies; in turn, these currencies were used mainly in conjunction with FSO loans to the countries that contributed them. In connection with the Second Replenishment, the four more-developed countries in Group A (Argentina, Brazil, Mexico, and Venezuela) agreed that a portion of their contributions could be made available to cover local costs in other borrowing countries, in addition to financing imports under IDB projects. Chile and Colombia were added to this list during the Third Replenishment. The Fourth Replenishment in 1975 marked a turning point in that all contributions to the FSO were required to be in convertible currencies.

The terms for borrowing under the FSO had initially stipulated servicing in local currencies (in addition to longer maturities and lower interest rates). These terms were hardened in connection with the Third Replenishment so that beginning in 1972 loans were serviced in the currencies disbursed rather than in local currencies. All FSO loans approved after 1977 are serviced in currencies disbursed.

A review of the first ten years of operations was carried out during the Third Replenishment. The FSO had granted nearly one-half of its loans to Group A countries; only 25 percent was distributed to the least-developed Group D countries (Bolivia, Dominican Republic, Ecuador, El Salvador, Guatemala, Haiti, Honduras, Nicaragua, and Paraguay) (IDB, *Annual Report*, 1972, 137–139). A double criterion, applied to assess eligibility, created this distribution; low-income countries were given preferential access but so were social projects in other borrowers. The Third Replenishment stipulated new policy guidelines establishing "strengthened emphasis on granting soft loans to the relatively less developed countries" in Groups C and D. This was accompanied by granting priority to the more-developed countries in relation to the ordinary capital resources (IDB, *Proposal for an Increase*, 1970).

In sum, two important policy changes were introduced in the early 1970s in connection with concessional lending: priority was given to low-income countries and repayment in local currencies ended. Lower interest rates and longer grace and amortization periods were established, bringing FSO terms closer to those offered by IDA: a ten-year grace period with forty years maturity. Interest rates varied between 1 and 4 percent, depending on the level of development of the country and the nature of the project. Concessional resources, which were equivalent to half of all resources during the 1960s, dwindled drastically over time despite the admission of new non-BMCs. By the Fourth Replenishment (1975–1978), they amounted to one-fourth of the replenishment and between 75 and 80 percent were allocated to Group D countries. At the Seventh Replenishment in 1989 they barely reached 1 percent, which was channeled solely to Group D.

The capital increase brought about by the Eighth Replenishment in 1994 raised a larger share of soft funding, $1 billion in new contributions to the FSO in the context of a $40 billion capital increase, a volume that allowed the Bank to lend indefinitely up to $7 billion a year without the financial support of a further capital increase. This is known in development banking circles as a sustainable level of lending (SLL).

In view of the paucity of concessional resources, a third window was created on the occasion of the Sixth Replenishment. An interest-subsidizing mechanism, the Intermediary Financing Facility (IFF), was created in 1983 with an initial appropriation of $61 million in convertible currencies from the general reserve of the FSO, with subsequent annual appropriations of approximately $15 million from the general reserve of the Fund, for a period of twenty years. This third window has been made available only to Group C and D countries to subsidize a maximum of five percentage points on ordinary capital loans.

The IDB has also administered funds provided under special conditions. The first trust fund, the Social Progress Trust Fund (SPTF), was created by the United States in 1961 in the context of the Alliance for Progress. Today the SPTF is a dwindling fund. Repayments of old loans are used to finance technical cooperation, and each operation requires U.S. approval. Also, under the terms established by the United States, the Bank makes periodic transfers to the Inter-American Foundation. For cash management purposes, if the Inter-American Foundation does not make full use of the funds at its disposal, the Bank uses the available funds through FSO loan disbursements, thereby providing the SPTF with additional income.

Other nonborrowing countries established funds of their own, in some cases before becoming members. The Canadian and the British funds provided tied capital at concessional terms. Switzerland, Norway, and Sweden provided funds for small projects and microenterprises to benefit low-income groups. The Belgian, Italian, and Portuguese governments created trust funds that are used to hire consultants from the member country. In 1988 Japan contributed Y13,500 million (approximately $136 million) to the Japan Special Fund (JSF) to finance nonreimbursable technical cooperation, primarily for project preparation, small projects, and emergency assistance to cope with natural disasters. In 1991 Japan committed Y353 million (approximately $3 million) to fund development-related, postgraduate studies in the region. In 1993 the Japanese government committed another Y1,500 million (approximately $15 million) to the JSF and, as a new form of cooperation, Y1,000 million (approximately $9 million) specifically for environment-related technical assistance. The JSF is presently the most generous of all trust funds operating at the IDB.

These trust funds make an important contribution to available resources, augmenting the Bank's resources by approximately $1.2 billion (IDB, *Annual Report*, 1992), but they have led to the inefficiencies associated with tied aid. Besides the administrative burden these funds pose, there is a growing trend toward consultancy funds earmarked for nationals of the non-BMC. After the SPTF was established by the United States, all later funds have come from smaller non-BMCs. The number of funds has increased noticeably since 1991 as the Bank gained stature in the eyes of nonborrowing members. Trust funds allow smaller non-BMCs to address their lending priorities or

pet issues more directly than during the course of replenishment negotiations when the search for a consensus limits their individual leverage. Although trust funds can contribute additional funds to the Bank,
they imply a potential erosion of multilateralism. It would, therefore,
be desirable to consolidate and streamline the various trust funds into
one single mechanism to improve efficiency and transparency.

## Country Allocations

The Bank has always worked with allocation guidelines for each country grouping. In order to guide access to resources as well as contributions to the Bank, BMCs were categorized into four groups, known as
A, B, C, and D (see Table 3.2). Nine indicators were used as yardsticks
of development: GNP, GNP per capita, population, annual rate of population growth, share of investment in GNP, rate of growth of per capita GNP, life expectancy at birth, infant mortality rates, and literacy
rates. After this first step, some adjustments and political compromises were needed to accommodate particular exigencies (IDB, *Impacto*,
1975).

At the Seventh Replenishment, the Bank limited loans to Group A
countries (Argentina, Mexico, Brazil, and Venezuela) and Group B
countries (Chile, Colombia, and Peru) to 65 percent over the 1990–1993
period in order to ensure sufficient financing for the less-developed
countries. This agreement was maintained for the Eighth Replenishment. In addition, all FSO resources are to be allocated over the
1994–1997 period to the five poorest Group D countries (Bolivia,
Guyana, Haiti, Honduras, and Nicaragua) and to the Caribbean
Development Bank for on-lending to eligible nonmembers of the IDB
(for example, the microstates of the Eastern Caribbean). The lending
program is not subject to any individual country allocation (see Table
3.3).

In contrast to the World Bank with its global field of operations
and shifting country priorities, IDB's lending policy has been steadily
and consistently involved in every BMC. "From the very beginning of
its operations, the IDB has recognized that one of its characteristic
activities must be to maintain a presence in all its member countries,
except where a country explicitly rejects it" (C. Morales in Calvo and
Tomassini 1970, 203). In countries that lack prepared projects or effective implementation, the regional bank, following its mandate, can
provide technical assistance to new projects. Lending to Groups C and
D countries is supported by more technical assistance in project preparation.

However, political pressures occasionally militate against this policy. During the three years that Salvador Allende was in power, lend-

**Table 3.2  IDB: Country Lending (annual average in U.S.$ millions)**

| Group | 1970–1972 OC | 1970–1972 FSO | 1973–1975 OC | 1973–1975 FSO | 1976–1978 OC | 1976–1978 FSO | 1979–1981 OC | 1979–1981 FSO | 1982–1984 OC | 1982–1984 FSO | 1985–1987 OC | 1985–1987 FSO | 1988–1990 OC | 1988–1990 FSO | 1991–1992 OC | 1991–1992 FSO | 1970–1992 Average OC | 1970–1992 Average FSO |
|---|---|---|---|---|---|---|---|---|---|---|---|---|---|---|---|---|---|---|
| **A** | | | | | | | | | | | | | | | | | | |
| Argentina | 84.3 | 30.0 | 75.3 | 40.0 | 219.7 | 34.0 | 283.1 | 16.5 | 267.4 | 43.2 | 201.4 | 0.0 | 176.3 | 0.0 | 928.1 | 36.4 | 236.2 | 24.3 |
| Brazil | 100.3 | 64.7 | 192.4 | 43.3 | 240.5 | 37.3 | 255.9 | 64.2 | 270.9 | 58.3 | 354.4 | 35.5 | 284.4 | 16.9 | 734.3 | 122.5 | 275.5 | 50.9 |
| Mexico | 36.9 | 49.6 | 110.7 | 44.0 | 218.0 | 3.3 | 255.3 | 12.5 | 254.9 | 20.7 | 286.8 | 7.6 | 432.0 | 0.2 | 600.0 | 0.0 | 252.6 | 18.4 |
| Venezuela | 26.9 | 31.8 | 0.0 | 14.4 | 0.0 | 0.0 | 0.0 | 0.0 | 159.4 | 0.0 | 131.9 | 1.8 | 303.0 | 0.2 | 376.6 | 0.0 | 107.9 | 6.4 |
| Subtotal | 248.4 | 176.1 | 378.4 | 141.7 | 678.2 | 74.6 | 794.3 | 93.2 | 952.6 | 122.2 | 974.5 | 44.9 | 1,195.7 | 17.3 | 2,639.0 | 158.9 | 872.2 | 99.9 |
| **B** | | | | | | | | | | | | | | | | | | |
| Chile | 0.0 | 4.9 | 40.3 | 15.7 | 32.7 | 15.2 | 48.6 | 0.0 | 380.9 | 0.0 | 294.1 | 0.0 | 340.9 | 0.0 | 202.3 | 0.0 | 165.2 | 4.8 |
| Colombia | 28.1 | 22.7 | 45.3 | 15.2 | 39.0 | 91.2 | 92.5 | 103.7 | 320.9 | 14.2 | 341.8 | 2.5 | 211.9 | 23.3 | 367.5 | 0.0 | 168.4 | 36.4 |
| Peru | 0.2 | 27.4 | 10.8 | 17.1 | 31.7 | 31.3 | 113.5 | 61.6 | 179.0 | 19.7 | 20.2 | 0.0 | 0.0 | 0.0 | 430.9 | 0.0 | 76.1 | 20.9 |
| Subtotal | 28.3 | 55.0 | 96.4 | 48.0 | 103.4 | 137.7 | 254.6 | 165.3 | 880.8 | 33.9 | 656.1 | 2.5 | 552.8 | 23.3 | 1,000.7 | 0.0 | 409.7 | 62.1 |
| **C** | | | | | | | | | | | | | | | | | | |
| Bahamas | 0.0 | 0.0 | 0.0 | 0.0 | 0.0 | 0.0 | 1.1 | 0.2 | 0.0 | 0.1 | 0.0 | 0.0 | 36.3 | 0.0 | 26.4 | 0.0 | 6.7 | 0.0 |
| Barbados | 0.0 | 1.3 | 3.0 | 3.2 | 0.5 | 3.0 | 3.1 | 5.1 | 9.8 | 1.7 | 9.9 | 2.4 | 3.1 | 0.0 | 34.9 | 0.0 | 6.2 | 2.2 |
| Costa Rica | 0.7 | 8.4 | 18.5 | 17.4 | 13.7 | 43.9 | 39.1 | 26.3 | 31.4 | 29.9 | 93.6 | 0.0 | 77.5 | 0.8 | 65.5 | 0.0 | 41.0 | 16.9 |
| Jamaica | 0.7 | 6.0 | 3.8 | 13.6 | 4.8 | 10.6 | 31.6 | 15.4 | 28.5 | 8.7 | 32.1 | 9.1 | 14.7 | 14.7 | 69.5 | 0.0 | 20.1 | 10.4 |
| Trinidad and Tobago | 0.4 | 7.7 | 0.0 | 2.6 | 0.0 | 0.0 | 0.0 | 0.0 | 0.0 | 0.0 | 18.2 | 2.3 | 32.2 | 1.1 | 145.8 | 2.0 | 16.5 | 2.0 |
| Uruguay | 8.0 | 4.5 | 13.8 | 6.2 | 15.1 | 0.0 | 57.2 | 0.2 | 46.8 | 12.6 | 80.5 | 8.2 | 20.3 | 0.3 | 214.8 | 0.0 | 46.5 | 4.3 |
| Subtotal | 9.8 | 27.9 | 39.1 | 43.0 | 34.1 | 57.5 | 132.1 | 47.2 | 116.5 | 53.0 | 234.3 | 22.0 | 184.1 | 16.9 | 556.9 | 2.0 | 137.1 | 35.8 |
| **D** | | | | | | | | | | | | | | | | | | |
| Bolivia | 6.7 | 11.8 | 15.5 | 33.1 | 15.6 | 85.1 | 32.2 | 14.1 | 50.2 | 59.8 | 71.0 | 4.3 | 91.7 | 53.9 | 97.5 | 40.2 | 44.2 | 37.6 |
| Dominican Republic | 0.0 | 11.3 | 12.2 | 24.8 | 0.0 | 31.5 | 15.4 | 83.9 | 101.3 | 50.9 | 95.2 | 0.2 | 35.6 | 20.7 | 0.0 | 31.9 | 34.6 | 31.9 |
| Ecuador | 3.3 | 27.0 | 15.4 | 25.9 | 35.6 | 44.7 | 73.3 | 72.7 | 107.3 | 56.9 | 187.4 | 50.8 | 26.8 | 49.6 | 146.9 | 0.0 | 69.7 | 43.7 |
| El Salvador | 0.0 | 17.2 | 0.0 | 28.1 | 5.0 | 29.2 | 5.6 | 44.9 | 65.7 | 12.3 | 0.0 | 66.1 | 13.3 | 26.3 | 155.5 | 42.0 | 22.3 | 32.7 |
| Guatemala | 0.0 | 3.1 | 8.3 | 38.9 | 0.0 | 34.0 | 28.3 | 32.0 | 45.5 | 30.5 | 81.1 | 19.5 | 0.0 | 14.7 | 0.0 | 32.5 | 21.8 | 25.2 |
| Guyana | 0.0 | 0.0 | 0.0 | 0.0 | 0.0 | 21.8 | 4.2 | 11.2 | 13.6 | 16.8 | 14.7 | 7.0 | 0.0 | 33.8 | 0.0 | 45.5 | 4.3 | 12.9 |
| Haiti | 0.0 | 5.7 | 0.0 | 21.1 | 0.0 | 21.1 | 0.0 | 4.7 | 0.0 | 16.8 | 0.0 | 26.9 | 0.0 | 18.8 | 0.0 | 6.2 | 0.0 | 16.1 |
| Honduras | 0.0 | 9.2 | 0.0 | 21.0 | 33.2 | 39.0 | 3.3 | 16.9 | 49.3 | 18.2 | 18.4 | 45.9 | 17.3 | 22.0 | 127.0 | 51.3 | 24.7 | 26.4 |
| Nicaragua | 0.0 | 9.5 | 0.0 | 18.7 | 1.0 | 32.3 | 0.3 | 36.6 | 21.9 | 18.2 | 18.4 | 0.0 | 0.0 | 0.0 | 46.6 | 88.3 | 6.2 | 18.8 |
| Panama | 0.0 | 11.6 | 0.0 | 25.0 | 29.3 | 17.6 | 29.1 | 36.1 | 45.4 | 7.4 | 48.8 | 7.3 | 0.0 | 0.0 | 64.7 | 0.0 | 24.7 | 14.0 |
| Paraguay | 0.0 | 13.0 | 0.0 | 17.4 | 85.0 | 13.6 | 5.9 | 25.0 | 25.4 | 36.4 | 6.7 | 4.1 | 0.0 | 115.7 | 140.0 | 35.9 | 25.7 | 32.4 |
| Surinam | 0.0 | 0.0 | 0.0 | 0.0 | 0.0 | 0.0 | 0.0 | 0.0 | 0.0 | 0.0 | 6.3 | 1.0 | 0.0 | 0.0 | 0.0 | 0.0 | 0.8 | 0.1 |
| Subtotal | 10.0 | 119.4 | 51.4 | 254.0 | 204.7 | 369.9 | 197.6 | 378.1 | 525.6 | 289.2 | 529.6 | 233.1 | 184.7 | 355.5 | 778.2 | 373.8 | 279.0 | 291.9 |
| Regional | 0.0 | 10.5 | 31.7 | 10.3 | 6.0 | 12.5 | 24.8 | 20.7 | 6.7 | 8.7 | 1.4 | 1.8 | 117.5 | 0.0 | 133.0 | 0.0 | 33.9 | 8.6 |
| Total | 296.5 | 388.9 | 597.0 | 497.0 | 1,026.4 | 652.2 | 1,403.4 | 704.5 | 2,482.2 | 507.0 | 2,395.9 | 304.3 | 2,234.8 | 413.0 | 5,107.8 | 534.7 | 1,732.0 | 498.3 |

*Source:* IDB, *Annual Reports,* various years.
*Notes:* OC: Ordinary Capital
FSO: Fund for Special Operations

Table 3.3 IDB: Country Lending (annual average in %)

| Group | 1970–1972 OC | 1970–1972 FSO | 1973–1975 OC | 1973–1975 FSO | 1976–1978 OC | 1976–1978 FSO | 1979–1981 OC | 1979–1981 FSO | 1982–1984 OC | 1982–1984 FSO | 1985–1987 OC | 1985–1987 FSO | 1988–1990 OC | 1988–1990 FSO | 1991–1992 OC | 1991–1992 FSO | 1970–1990 Average OC | 1970–1990 Average FSO |
|---|---|---|---|---|---|---|---|---|---|---|---|---|---|---|---|---|---|---|
| **A** | | | | | | | | | | | | | | | | | | |
| Argentina | 28.4 | 7.7 | 12.6 | 8.0 | 21.4 | 5.2 | 20.2 | 2.3 | 10.8 | 8.5 | 8.4 | 0.0 | 7.9 | 0.0 | 18.2 | 6.8 | 15.8 | 4.7 |
| Brazil | 33.8 | 16.6 | 32.2 | 8.7 | 23.4 | 5.7 | 18.2 | 9.1 | 10.9 | 11.5 | 14.8 | 11.7 | 12.7 | 4.1 | 14.4 | 22.9 | 20.4 | 10.5 |
| Mexico | 12.4 | 12.8 | 18.5 | 8.9 | 21.2 | 0.5 | 18.2 | 1.8 | 10.3 | 4.1 | 12.0 | 2.5 | 19.3 | 0.0 | 11.7 | 0.0 | 15.7 | 4.1 |
| Venezuela | 9.1 | 8.2 | 0.0 | 2.9 | 0.0 | 0.0 | 0.0 | 0.0 | 6.4 | 0.0 | 5.5 | 0.6 | 13.6 | 0.0 | 7.4 | 0.0 | 5.1 | 1.6 |
| Subtotal | 83.7 | 45.3 | 63.3 | 28.5 | 66.0 | 11.4 | 56.6 | 13.2 | 38.4 | 24.1 | 40.7 | 14.8 | 53.5 | 4.1 | 51.7 | 29.7 | 57.0 | 20.9 |
| **B** | | | | | | | | | | | | | | | | | | |
| Chile | 0.0 | 1.3 | 6.7 | 3.2 | 3.2 | 2.3 | 3.5 | 0.0 | 15.3 | 0.0 | 12.3 | 0.0 | 15.3 | 0.0 | 4.0 | 0.0 | 7.8 | 1.0 |
| Colombia | 9.5 | 5.8 | 7.6 | 3.1 | 3.8 | 14.0 | 6.6 | 14.7 | 12.9 | 2.8 | 14.3 | 0.8 | 9.5 | 5.6 | 7.2 | 0.0 | 9.0 | 6.2 |
| Peru | 0.1 | 7.0 | 1.8 | 3.4 | 3.1 | 4.8 | 8.1 | 8.7 | 7.2 | 3.9 | 0.8 | 0.0 | 0.0 | 0.0 | 8.4 | 0.0 | 3.4 | 3.7 |
| Subtotal | 9.6 | 14.1 | 16.1 | 9.7 | 10.1 | 21.1 | 18.2 | 23.4 | 35.4 | 6.7 | 27.4 | 0.8 | 24.8 | 5.6 | 19.6 | 0.0 | 20.2 | 10.9 |
| **C** | | | | | | | | | | | | | | | | | | |
| Bahamas | 0.0 | 0.0 | 0.0 | 0.0 | 0.0 | 0.0 | 0.1 | 0.0 | 0.0 | 0.0 | 0.0 | 0.0 | 1.6 | 0.0 | 0.5 | 0.0 | 0.3 | 0.0 |
| Barbados | 0.0 | 0.3 | 0.5 | 0.7 | 0.0 | 0.5 | 0.2 | 0.7 | 0.4 | 0.3 | 0.4 | 0.8 | 0.1 | 0.0 | 0.7 | 0.0 | 0.3 | 0.4 |
| Costa Rica | 0.2 | 2.2 | 3.1 | 3.5 | 1.3 | 6.7 | 2.8 | 3.7 | 1.3 | 5.9 | 3.9 | 0.0 | 3.5 | 0.2 | 1.3 | 0.0 | 2.2 | 3.0 |
| Jamaica | 0.2 | 1.6 | 0.6 | 2.7 | 0.5 | 1.6 | 2.2 | 2.2 | 1.1 | 1.7 | 1.3 | 3.0 | 0.7 | 3.6 | 1.4 | 0.0 | 1.0 | 2.2 |
| Trinidad and Tobago | 0.1 | 2.0 | 0.0 | 0.5 | 0.0 | 0.0 | 0.0 | 0.0 | 0.0 | 0.0 | 0.8 | 0.8 | 1.4 | 0.3 | 2.9 | 0.4 | 0.5 | 0.4 |
| Uruguay | 2.7 | 1.1 | 2.3 | 1.2 | 1.5 | 0.0 | 4.1 | 0.0 | 1.9 | 2.5 | 3.4 | 2.7 | 0.9 | 0.1 | 4.2 | 0.0 | 2.5 | 1.0 |
| Subtotal | 3.2 | 7.2 | 6.5 | 8.6 | 3.3 | 8.8 | 9.4 | 6.6 | 4.7 | 10.4 | 9.8 | 7.3 | 8.2 | 4.2 | 11.0 | 0.4 | 6.8 | 7.0 |
| **D** | | | | | | | | | | | | | | | | | | |
| Bolivia | 2.2 | 3.0 | 2.6 | 6.7 | 1.5 | 13.1 | 2.3 | 2.0 | 2.0 | 11.8 | 3.0 | 1.4 | 4.1 | 13.1 | 1.9 | 7.5 | 2.5 | 7.3 |
| Dominican Republic | 0.0 | 2.9 | 2.0 | 5.0 | 0.0 | 4.8 | 1.1 | 11.9 | 4.1 | 10.0 | 4.0 | 0.1 | 1.6 | 5.0 | 0.0 | 6.0 | 1.7 | 5.7 |
| Ecuador | 1.1 | 6.9 | 2.6 | 5.2 | 3.5 | 6.9 | 5.2 | 10.3 | 4.3 | 11.2 | 7.8 | 16.7 | 1.2 | 12.0 | 2.9 | 0.0 | 3.6 | 9.2 |
| El Salvador | 0.0 | 4.4 | 0.0 | 5.7 | 0.5 | 4.5 | 0.4 | 6.4 | 2.6 | 2.4 | 0.0 | 21.7 | 0.6 | 6.4 | 3.0 | 7.9 | 0.7 | 7.4 |
| Guatemala | 0.0 | 0.8 | 1.4 | 7.8 | 0.0 | 5.2 | 2.0 | 4.5 | 1.8 | 6.0 | 3.4 | 6.4 | 0.0 | 3.6 | 0.0 | 6.1 | 1.1 | 5.0 |
| Guyana | 0.0 | 0.0 | 0.0 | 0.0 | 0.0 | 3.3 | 0.3 | 1.6 | 0.5 | 0.0 | 0.6 | 2.3 | 0.0 | 8.2 | 0.0 | 8.5 | 0.2 | 2.6 |
| Haiti | 0.0 | 1.5 | 0.0 | 4.2 | 0.0 | 3.2 | 0.0 | 0.7 | 0.0 | 3.3 | 0.0 | 8.8 | 0.0 | 4.6 | 0.0 | 1.2 | 0.0 | 3.6 |
| Honduras | 0.0 | 2.4 | 0.0 | 4.2 | 3.2 | 6.0 | 0.2 | 2.4 | 2.0 | 3.6 | 0.8 | 15.1 | 0.8 | 5.3 | 2.5 | 9.6 | 1.1 | 5.8 |
| Nicaragua | 0.0 | 2.4 | 0.0 | 3.8 | 0.1 | 4.9 | 0.0 | 5.2 | 0.9 | 0.0 | 0.0 | 0.0 | 0.0 | 0.0 | 0.9 | 16.5 | 0.2 | 3.3 |
| Panama | 0.0 | 3.0 | 0.0 | 5.0 | 2.9 | 2.7 | 2.1 | 5.1 | 1.8 | 1.5 | 2.0 | 2.4 | 0.0 | 0.0 | 1.3 | 0.0 | 1.3 | 2.6 |
| Paraguay | 0.0 | 3.3 | 0.0 | 3.5 | 8.3 | 2.1 | 0.4 | 3.5 | 1.0 | 7.2 | 0.3 | 1.3 | 0.0 | 28.0 | 2.7 | 6.7 | 1.5 | 7.0 |
| Surinam | 0.0 | 0.0 | 0.0 | 0.0 | 0.0 | 0.0 | 0.0 | 0.0 | 0.0 | 0.0 | 0.3 | 0.3 | 0.0 | 0.0 | 0.0 | 0.0 | 0.1 | 0.1 |
| Subtotal | 3.3 | 30.6 | 8.6 | 51.1 | 20.0 | 56.7 | 14.0 | 53.6 | 21.0 | 57.0 | 22.2 | 76.5 | 8.3 | 86.2 | 15.2 | 70.0 | 14.0 | 59.6 |
| Regional | 0.0 | 2.7 | 5.3 | 2.1 | 0.6 | 1.9 | 1.8 | 2.9 | 0.3 | 1.7 | 0.1 | 0.6 | 5.3 | 0.0 | 2.6 | 0.0 | 2.0 | 1.6 |
| Total[a] | 100.0 | 100.0 | 100.0 | 100.0 | 100.0 | 100.0 | 100.0 | 100.0 | 100.0 | 100.0 | 100.0 | 100.0 | 100.0 | 100.0 | 100.0 | 100.0 | 100.0 | 100.0 |

*Source:* IDB, *Annual Reports.*
*Notes:* OC: Ordinary Capital
FSO: Fund for Special Operations
a Totals have been rounded to 100.

ing to Chile out of ordinary capital resources was halted due to pressure from the United States (U.S. Treasury 1982). Only the private sector received funding. Two loans were approved from the FSO in 1971 to private universities in Santiago and Valdivia. Confrontation with the United States also impeded the processing of loans to Nicaragua during the Sandinista regime[8] and to Panama at the end of the 1980s when the United States tried to oust the Noriega regime. Both these countries subsequently fell into arrears, at which point arrears policy was applicable; in other words, no new commitments were made (disbursements are suspended when arrears exceed thirty days, and new project appraisal is suspended after six months arrears). Nicaragua subsequently cleared arrears in 1991 and Panama in 1992.

It is important to note that until the Eighth Replenishment, the U.S. executive director had to be present for a quorum at the Board, thus exercising an implicit veto. Borrowing member countries also avoided open confrontation with donors. The voting procedures of the Bank have acted as safeguards for non-BMCs, rather than the primary means whereby acquiescence is secured. The new decisionmaking procedures have made the safeguards more transparent, but, for the most part, BMCs still prefer not to force a vote. Costa Rica, for example, faced with conflict over land demanded by U.S. nationals, chose to postpone presentation of a proposal to the Board to avoid confrontation and the formal deferral mechanism.

The end of the Cold War has pushed democratic rule to the top of international concerns. After the fall of President Aristide in Haiti, the Bank suspended all further country planning. When President Fujimori of Peru suspended constitutional rule in April 1992, the IDB blocked new loans to the country and froze the signature of loans already approved by the Board. The block was lifted in September when elections were announced. The Bank subsequently led an international rescue package for Peru.

The extent of the Bank's policy commitment in all countries can be gauged in Tables 3.2 and 3.3, which reflect the country distribution of the lending program. As can be seen, about 50 percent of the program has been absorbed by the more-developed countries in Group A while 20 percent has gone to the least-developed countries in Group D. Group D captures over 50 percent of the funds of the soft window. Distribution within the country groupings is fairly even, with a few exceptions. Venezuela is below average in Group A, having suspended borrowings during the oil bonanza in the 1970s. Peru in Group B fell below average in the late 1980s because it suspended debt servicing and the arrears policy was applied.[9] In this group, Colombia has been an active recipient both of hard and soft funds. The same is true of Costa Rica, which outpaced Uruguay, in Group C. In Group D, the major overall recipients are Bolivia and Ecuador, which together with Honduras have been major recipients of soft loans. It is noteworthy that the IDB continued lending to El Salvador through the war years in the 1980s.

Small countries, in order to increase their access to resources, are granted a higher share of foreign exchange financing for project costs besides their funding allocation. This distribution of foreign and local funding is known as the matrix. It was set along a continuum for the different country groupings in the Seventh and Eighth Replenishments. The share of total costs financed by Bank lending is now 50 percent for Group A countries, 60 percent for Group B countries, 70 percent for Group C countries, and 80 percent for Group D countries. In order to fulfill the policy mandated at the Fifth Replenishment to direct at least 50 percent of the net benefits of projects to low-income beneficiaries, an additional ten percentage points of foreign exchange financing was allowed as a financial incentive. The incentive has been maintained for the poverty reduction goal of the Eighth Replenishment. This incentive is available to projects or programs to benefit the poor.

The Bank does not have a "graduation" policy. Given that present levels of capital inflows may not be sustainable, graduation could make more funding available to the remaining borrowers. A graduation policy, however, would need to be accompanied by country risk analysis to design lending programs that correspond with fluctuating conditions in international markets and with the country's changing debt profile. Although absorptive capacities still vary widely, the rapid cycles of overlending and underlending from capital markets can quickly reverse the debt profiles of BMCs. The financial liberalization of most BMCs has also made their performance more sensitive to changes in the interest rate policies of the G-7 countries. The new context in which the Bank and its BMCs operate warrants close monitoring of debt profiles. The move to a sustainable level of lending operation would also require moving away from preset allocations.

## Sectoral Distribution

In its first decade the IDB concentrated mainly on lending to directly productive sectors; agriculture, industry, and mining absorbed over 40 percent of lending. Infrastructure (electric power, transportation, and communications) came second with a further 30 percent. Social development projects involving water supply and sewerage systems, urban development and housing, and education accounted for nearly 25 percent of the total. Nonetheless, the social dimension of IDB lending has

Table 3.4   Sectoral Lending (annual average in U.S.$ millions)

| | 1970–1972 | | 1973–1975 | | 1976–1978 | | 1979–1981 | | 1982–1984 | | 1985–1987 | | 1988–1990 | | 1991–1992 | |
|---|---|---|---|---|---|---|---|---|---|---|---|---|---|---|---|---|
| | IDB | WB | IDB | WB | IDB | WB | IDB | WB | IDB | WB | IDB | WB | IDB | WB | IDB | WB |
| Agriculture | 459 | 192 | 747 | 833 | 1,023 | 1,496 | 1,990 | 1,900 | 1,768 | 2,006 | 1,619 | 2,135 | 1,291 | 2,244 | 631 | 1,311 |
| Industry | 255 | 302 | 455 | 320 | 1,070 | 753 | 613 | 1,023 | 1,848 | 1,415 | 1,198 | 811 | 457 | 575 | 297 | 200 |
| Tourism | 26 | 22 | 36 | 0 | 82 | 42 | 4 | 53 | 155 | 0 | 203 | 0 | 124 | 0 | 0 | 0 |
| Energy | 484 | 643 | 904 | 422 | 1,402 | 1,066 | 1,936 | 2,190 | 2,664 | 737 | 2,208 | 2,394 | 1,962 | 1,001 | 411 | 299 |
| Transport | 458 | 825 | 633 | 751 | 587 | 980 | 1,090 | 1,582 | 741 | 1,451 | 1,036 | 1,874 | 1,248 | 816 | 1,472 | 678 |
| Subtotal | 1,682 | 1,984 | 2,775 | 2,326 | 4,164 | 4,337 | 5,633 | 6,748 | 7,176 | 5,609 | 6,264 | 7,214 | 5,082 | 4,636 | 2,811 | 2,488 |
| Sanitation | 142 | 160 | 266 | 231 | 507 | 281 | 680 | 896 | 781 | 622 | 1,085 | 451 | 1,019 | 1,369 | 969 | 852 |
| Education | 110 | 46 | 181 | 107 | 259 | 110 | 252 | 270 | 475 | 116 | 380 | 307 | 238 | 148 | 424 | 1,381 |
| Urban Development | 81 | 0 | 62 | 43 | 73 | 105 | 53 | 407 | 526 | 360 | 471 | 776 | 537 | 1,714 | 194 | 594 |
| Ecology | — | — | — | — | — | — | — | — | — | — | — | — | — | — | 622 | 498 |
| Social Global | — | — | — | — | — | — | — | — | — | — | — | — | — | — | 93 | 167 |
| Subtotal | 333 | 206 | 509 | 381 | 839 | 496 | 985 | 1,573 | 1,782 | 1,098 | 1,936 | 1,534 | 1,794 | 3,231 | 2,302 | 3,492 |
| Export Finance | 52 | 60 | 48 | 0 | 121 | 0 | 174 | 37 | 201 | 786 | 224 | 297 | 223 | 30 | 0 | 0 |
| Preinvestment | 36 | 0 | 48 | 0 | 83 | 0 | 57 | 0 | 151 | 0 | 80 | 0 | 31 | 0 | 30 | 0 |
| Other | 0 | 61 | 0 | 98 | 0 | 349 | 99 | 362 | 46 | 941 | 21 | 2,327 | 1,051 | 480 | 51 | 0 |
| Policy | 0 | 0 | 0 | 0 | 0 | 0 | 0 | 50 | 0 | 252 | 0 | 3,423 | 0 | 4,490 | 6,195 | 4,915 |
| Subtotal | 88 | 121 | 96 | 98 | 204 | 349 | 330 | 449 | 398 | 1,979 | 325 | 6,047 | 1,305 | 5,000 | 6,276 | 4,915 |
| Total | 2,103 | 2,311 | 3,380 | 2,805 | 5,207 | 5,182 | 6,948 | 8,770 | 9,356 | 8,686 | 8,525 | 14,795 | 8,181 | 12,867 | 11,389 | 10,895 |

Source: IDB, Annual Reports. WB, Statement of Loans.
Note: WB figures relate only to IDB borrowers.
These figures are greater than those in Table 6.2 because they include "hybrid" loans or policy-based investment loans.

Table 3.5  Sectoral Lending (annual average in %)

| | 1970–1972 | | 1973–1975 | | 1976–1978 | | 1979–1981 | | 1982–1984 | | 1985–1987 | | 1988–1990 | | 1991–1992 | |
|---|---|---|---|---|---|---|---|---|---|---|---|---|---|---|---|---|
| | IDB | WB | IDB | WB | IDB | WB | IDB | WB | IDB | WB | IDB | WB | IDB | WB | IDB | WB |
| Agriculture | 21.8 | 8.3 | 22.2 | 29.7 | 19.6 | 28.9 | 29.1 | 21.7 | 18.7 | 23.1 | 18.0 | 14.4 | 15.8 | 17.4 | 5.5 | 12.0 |
| Industry | 12.2 | 13.1 | 13.5 | 11.4 | 20.5 | 14.5 | 9.0 | 11.7 | 19.5 | 16.3 | 14.2 | 5.5 | 5.6 | 4.5 | 2.6 | 1.8 |
| Tourism | 1.2 | 1.0 | 1.1 | 0.0 | 1.6 | 0.8 | 0.1 | 0.6 | 1.6 | 0.0 | 2.4 | 0.0 | 1.5 | 0.0 | 0.0 | 0.0 |
| Energy | 23.0 | 27.8 | 26.8 | 15.0 | 26.9 | 20.6 | 28.3 | 25.0 | 28.2 | 8.5 | 26.2 | 16.2 | 24.0 | 7.8 | 3.6 | 2.7 |
| Transport | 21.8 | 35.7 | 18.8 | 26.8 | 11.3 | 18.9 | 15.9 | 18.0 | 7.8 | 16.7 | 12.3 | 12.7 | 15.3 | 6.3 | 12.9 | 6.2 |
| Subtotal | 80.0 | 85.9 | 82.4 | 82.9 | 79.9 | 83.7 | 82.4 | 77.0 | 75.8 | 64.6 | 73.1 | 48.8 | 62.2 | 36.0 | 24.6 | 22.7 |
| Sanitation | 6.7 | 6.9 | 7.9 | 8.2 | 9.7 | 5.4 | 8.5 | 10.2 | 8.3 | 7.2 | 12.9 | 3.0 | 12.5 | 10.6 | 8.5 | 7.8 |
| Education | 5.2 | 2.0 | 5.4 | 3.8 | 5.0 | 2.1 | 3.7 | 3.1 | 5.0 | 1.3 | 4.5 | 2.1 | 2.9 | 1.2 | 3.7 | 12.7 |
| Urban Development | 3.8 | 0.0 | 1.5 | 1.5 | 1.4 | 2.0 | 0.8 | 4.6 | 6.6 | 4.1 | 5.6 | 5.2 | 6.6 | 13.3 | 1.7 | 5.5 |
| Ecology | – | – | – | – | – | – | – | – | – | – | – | – | – | – | 5.5 | 4.6 |
| Social Global | – | – | – | – | – | – | – | – | – | – | – | – | – | – | 0.8 | 1.5 |
| Subtotal | 15.7 | 8.9 | 14.8 | 13.5 | 16.1 | 9.5 | 13.0 | 17.9 | 19.9 | 12.6 | 23.0 | 10.3 | 22.0 | 25.1 | 20.2 | 32.1 |
| Export Finance | 2.5 | 2.6 | 1.4 | 0.0 | 2.3 | 0.0 | 2.5 | 0.4 | 2.1 | 9.0 | 2.7 | 2.0 | 2.7 | 0.2 | 0.0 | 0.0 |
| Preinvestment | 1.7 | 0.0 | 1.4 | 0.0 | 1.6 | 0.0 | 0.8 | 0.0 | 1.6 | 0.0 | 0.9 | 0.0 | 0.4 | 0.0 | 0.3 | 0.0 |
| Other | 0.0 | 2.6 | 0.0 | 3.5 | 0.0 | 6.7 | 1.4 | 4.1 | 0.5 | 10.8 | 0.2 | 15.7 | 12.8 | 3.7 | 0.4 | 0.0 |
| Policy | 0.0 | 0.0 | 0.0 | 0.0 | 0.0 | 0.0 | 0.0 | 0.6 | 0.0 | 2.9 | 0.0 | 23.1 | 0.0 | 34.9 | 54.4 | 45.1 |
| Subtotal | 4.2 | 5.2 | 2.8 | 3.5 | 3.9 | 6.7 | 4.7 | 5.1 | 4.2 | 22.7 | 3.8 | 40.8 | 15.9 | 38.8 | 55.1 | 45.1 |
| Total | 100 | 100 | 100 | 100 | 100 | 100 | 100 | 100 | 100 | 100 | 100 | 100 | 100 | 100 | 100 | 100 |

*Source:* IDB, *Annual Reports.* WB, *Statement of Loans.*
*Note:* WB figures relate only to IDB borrowers.
These figures are greater than those in Table 6.2 because they include "hybrid" loans or policy-based investment loans.

been and is more important than is reflected in its proportion of resources. Typically these projects are small in terms of funding. The IDB was the source of nearly two-thirds of all external investments in potable water during the 1960s and 1970s. The World Bank entered into this sector in the 1980s, but the IDB maintained its lead (see Tables 3.4 and 3.5). This original sectoral distribution of IDB funds represented a marked contrast with the pattern of World Bank lending until then. Indeed, 90 percent of World Bank loans to Latin America were then for electric power and transportation (Dell 1972).

Several reasons account for the differences between the sectoral distributions of World Bank and IDB loans. In the first place, a large proportion of IDB loans were made first to private firms, either directly or indirectly through DFIs. This was possible for the IDB because, according to the terms of its Articles of Agreement, it does not need government guarantees. It is empowered to accept guarantees by private banks or DFIs.

As a regional bank with a comprehensive network of field offices, the IDB acquired a high degree of familiarity with the local business community and market conditions. Thus, it was better equipped to handle the small financing requirements of private agents. An initial de facto division of labor emerged whereby the World Bank concentrated on the large-scale loans, such as those required for infrastructure projects. Infrastructure, especially power projects, offered a convenient way of transferring external resources. In the early 1960s, the United States was another key provider of development assistance to Latin America and the Caribbean.

At each replenishment the IDB has been mandated to observe sector allocations. However, the World Bank does not work under such guidelines, and by the end of the 1960s, this division of labor had eroded. The World Bank entered into productive and social projects, and the IDB initiated the funding of large-scale projects in infrastructure. The differentiation between the IDB and the World Bank diminished further during the 1970s up to the debt crisis. Both banks became heavily involved in power supply and transportation with roughly one-half of their lending, although the IDB was more inclined toward energy resources and the World Bank toward transportation. The World Bank remained the most important external source of funding to the sector, even though funding was halved at the end of the 1980s.

By the Fifth Replenishment in 1979, energy resources had been identified as the major bottleneck in development (IDB, *Annual Report*, 1979, 10). Support for energy resources, which had represented about 14 percent of total lending in the 1960s, rose to 25 percent in the 1970s and 1980s. Flows of funds into energy projects from the IDB have consistently surpassed those from the World Bank. They peaked during the period of the Sixth Replenishment (1982–1986) and declined in absolute terms thereafter.

The IDB was the major external source of rural credit in Latin America. In the first twenty years, about one-quarter of all lending was directed to specific agricultural projects. If, in addition, account is taken of infrastructure projects in rural areas (housing, water supply, roads, and power) as well as technical assistance, the resources allocated to rural development amount to over one-third. The guidelines for the Fifth Replenishment drawn up in 1979 established that 30 to 35 percent of lending should go to the rural sector during 1979–1982, primarily to improve social services and to stimulate production, a target that the Bank accomplished.

The World Bank caught up with the IDB in the mid-1970s when its loans to agriculture increased fourfold and represented one-third of its lending to the region. This share declined in the 1980s when both banks had even shares of agriculture in their portfolios. By the end of the decade, World Bank absolute flows were almost double those of the IDB, and agriculture represented a little over 15 percent of both banks' lending to the region.

Since its Fifth Replenishment, the Bank has had another target: 50 percent of the lending program should benefit low-income groups. No other multilateral development bank has such a quantitative target. The requirement was pushed strongly by the Carter administration.[10] It covered loan benefits across all types of loans rather than projects of social development per se, so these did not necessarily become objects of special attention.

With the IDB's shift into infrastructure in the 1970s, lending to social sectors suffered, decreasing to 15 percent—down from nearly 25 percent of total lending in the 1960s. Nonetheless, in absolute terms until the end of the 1970s, the IDB was still the major source of external funding for projects of social development. Positions were then reversed, when World Bank funding to social sectors reflected its "basic human needs" activism. Transfers increased threefold in the 1979–1981 period and surpassed those from the IDB for the first time.

In the subsequent six-year period, the IDB regained its ascendancy as lending to social sectors doubled throughout the debt crisis. Meanwhile, though social sector lending from the World Bank did not fall significantly in absolute terms, this represented a much reduced share (from 18 percent in 1979–1981 to 10 percent in 1985–1987) of its increased involvement in the region, most of which was concentrated in adjustment lending.

World Bank transfers to the region grew by 70 percent in 1985–1987. These funds were funneled mainly via policy-based lending reflecting priorities of the Baker Plan for debt relief. Policy-based lending absorbed one-fourth of World Bank transfers to the region. But by the end of the 1980s funding of social sectors regained ground and represented one-fourth of total World Bank lending—nearly double the amount of funding provided by the IDB. Within social sector lending, the IDB has provided more funds to sanitation, health, and education. In contrast, the World Bank focused on urban development starting from zero at the beginning of the 1970s to double the total IDB funding in the next two decades.

## Regional Economic Collapse

When the Bank first opened its doors, its operating style was largely influenced by a perception of the principal problems of its borrowing member countries: the need for resource transfers coupled with poor project preparation and execution. During its first fifteen years the IDB was at the forefront of innovative financial cooperation. Not only did it experiment in areas it considered a priority, but also, under its Articles of Agreement, in contrast to the World Bank, it could lend directly to the private sector without government guarantees.

The financial bonanza prompted by the recycling of oil-surplus funds demoted the IDB as a leading provider of capital to the region. Private banks that had barely contributed 2 percent of net inflows to IDB BMCs in the early 1960s contributed more than 50 percent of total inflows by the end of the 1970s. The Bank reacted by concentrating on megaprojects. The flow of funds into social projects, which had accounted for nearly 25 percent of total lending in the 1960s, fell to 15 percent in the 1970s. It should be noted that this shift was accompanied by a decline in concessional lending, which had started at half of the lending program and fell to a quarter by the end of the 1970s.

Access to international capital markets was temptingly easy for the private sector; borrowing from the IDB's ordinary capital was less attractive than borrowing from private capital markets or applying for suppliers' credits, and it was a less cumbersome process. It was estimated that it took an average of four years for a proposal to the IDB to culminate in actual disbursements. This failing was reflected in the IDB's declining support to the private sector, and particularly to industry. The Bank thus had a hard time fulfilling one of the basic objectives for which it had been established. Also, the Fifth Replenishment (1979) and the Sixth Replenishment (1982) guidelines had established a cap on lending to Group A countries precisely because of their access to private capital markets.[11]

The Bank, during its first decade, had been at the forefront of lending and of economic thought; however, the availability of competing sources of finance throughout the 1970s undermined the importance of the Bank to the more creditworthy countries. The access to private capital flows coincided with regionwide questioning of the founding ideas of the Bank; orthodox import substitution and government intervention as well as regional integration were viewed with increasing skepticism. Easy borrowing in international capital markets relieved the pressure to save foreign exchange through import substitution. Most of the regional cooperation schemes that had been launched in the previous decade faced profound institutional crises.

The Bank was also affected by this inertia. The IDB did not have the analytical or political resources to anticipate the changes in U.S. monetary policies. It had given some timid warnings that the recycling of petrodollars could become a mixed blessing. In a 1979 speech, President Antonio Ortiz Mena warned that the accumulation of debt had become explosive: whereas annual debt servicing had absorbed 14 percent of current export earnings up to 1976, by 1978 it had jumped to 25 percent.[12] In his speech to the 1979 annual meeting of governors in Kingston, Jamaica, he called attention to the uncertainty entailed by massive short-term financing of balance-of-payments deficits. Neither the governments nor the private banks heeded the signals, and the Bank was not empowered to take action.

When the debt crisis finally broke, the Bank was unprepared to cope with the longest and most severe setback suffered by the region. Disbursements increased during the second half of 1982 and in 1983 before declining sharply from 1984 to 1987.[13] Protracted delays in loan disbursements (an old problem) became painfully acute at this time. Dell's analysis of the IDB in the 1960s had already attributed part of the disbursement delay to the normal lags inherent in a project; but a substantial part was due also to the elaborate system of checks and controls used to reduce risks (Dell 1972, 245).

The new problems stem from the BMCs' indebtedness, budget cuts, lack of maintenance funds, and so on, which themselves lead to delays. The so-called flexible approach measures were introduced in 1983–1984 to maintain project implementation and disbursements when these were restricted as a consequence of cost increases or lack of pari passu funds.[14] The Bank was allowed to increase its share in project costs, including the financing of local costs; to reduce the physical size of projects and thereby accelerate disbursements; and to introduce investment loans to cover maintenance as well as new projects. These measures, however, speeded disbursements only partially and for a limited time, as the three country studies in Chapter 4 show. By 1988 there was a backlog of $10 billion.

Worst of all, the Bank was torn in the struggle between the Reagan administration and the highly indebted largest BMCs in Group A.

Together the United States and the four Group A countries accounted for nearly two-thirds of the voting power. The small countries were neglected in this debate.[15]

The region's debt owed to international financial institutions (the IMF, World Bank, and IDB) grew from a 6.4 percent of its total debt in 1980 to 15.6 percent in 1988 and a further three percentage points in 1990. Thus its share of total debt tripled in a decade. Honduras, Panama, and Peru were in arrears with the IMF, the World Bank, and the IDB; Nicaragua was in arrears with the IDB and the World Bank. Guyana was declared ineligible by the IMF in 1985, Peru in 1986, and Panama in 1989.[16]

By 1987 aggregate net multilateral flows from the IDB, World Bank, and IMF to the region were negative numbers. At the IDB, part of the problem was in the nature of project lending and the drying up of pari passu funding caused by fiscal distress. It was compounded by the unprecedented delay in agreement on the replenishment of the Bank's capital, which was due in 1987.

The Seventh Replenishment was needed to turn the IDB into an active provider of funds, for which substantially higher loan disbursements were required; this in turn required unlinking lending from project execution. An inherent part of the problem was achieving both quicker disbursements and tighter controls over the lending program. This led to controversy over a number of issues, mainly between the United States and the four highly indebted Group A countries. The United States did not trust any bank dominated by borrowers to carry out the conditionality of policy loans. It demanded an alteration of voting power for loan approval and, as an additional precaution, also required the IDB to work under the shelter of the World Bank's program. Other demands such as stricter country programming to guide lending and staffing concerns were easily accommodated.

Enrique Iglesias was elected president in 1988 with the short-term goal of moving the negotiations forward and the long-term mission of charting a future course for the Bank. The new president immediately set in motion an internal review process to lay the groundwork for a "new Inter-American Development Bank." He also called a high-level review committee to assist in planning the Bank's future. The committee, chaired by John Petty, reported at the end of 1988. It supported the already accepted view that policy-based loans were needed to overcome the rigidities of the project approach and restore inflows swiftly. For the overall program, the report recommended continuing the primary focus on public sector and social capital investment and increasing loans to the private sector and to export finance. It suggested a broadened concern for environmental protection by including this in every project at the design stage. An increase in technical cooperation was pinpointed as important to buttress the Bank's developmental function. The report suggested more than doubling the rate of spending in this area for a target of at least 5 percent of loans disbursed. The committee considered that a reappraisal of voting shares was timely to augment available resources to the Bank—although it did not recommend necessarily cutting back on the 53.76 percent voting share held by borrowers. To further enhance the multilateral character of the Bank, it also suggested an increase in nonregional representation among the staff.

The Bank was revitalized by the internal review exercise and the mending of bridges with non-BMCs. The Seventh Replenishment was finally agreed upon at the 1989 annual meeting. As a result of its new mandate the Bank abandoned its reactive position in favor of an active one vis-à-vis project selection. To guide its lending the Bank is required to produce a "country program," for which IDB management reviews the proposals made by national authorities "in the light of its own analysis of the country's economic situation, constraints to growth, the adequacy of macroeconomic and sectoral policies, the capabilities of relevant institutions" (IDB, *Proposal for the Sixth General Increase*, 1989, 16). The country programs are intended to improve coordination with the Bretton Woods institutions. The advent of country programming has been crucially important to the way in which the Bank now plans and organizes its assistance strategies.[17] The new Office of Strategic Planning is expected to carve out a distinctive role for the IDB, to lead to a clear statement of the Bank's overall goals, and to focus the dialogue with borrowing countries on poverty reduction and social equity.

As a result of these changes, the Bank was empowered, on one hand, to engage in policy-based lending (not to exceed 25 percent of total lending) to oversee adjustment; and on the other, to restore inflows into the region. To support the Brady Plan it has been authorized to provide a financing facility for debt and debt service reduction as a component of its adjustment lending program.

Greatly increased resources were channeled to the Bank, and a renewed sense of purpose was instilled. The Seventh Replenishment sustained a $22.5 billion lending program in 1990–1993, including $1.9 billion for the FSO and $1.1 billion under the IFF, which subsidizes interest rates on loans from the ordinary capital account with transfers from the net income of the FSO. However, the paid-in portion, 2.5 percent, was the lowest for any MDB at the time.[18] The previous replenishment, which was negotiated at the outbreak of the debt crisis, amounted to $15 billion, of which 4.5 percent had been paid in. As paid-in portions have declined with each replenishment, the Bank has

Figure 3.1    IDB and World Bank Commitments in Latin America

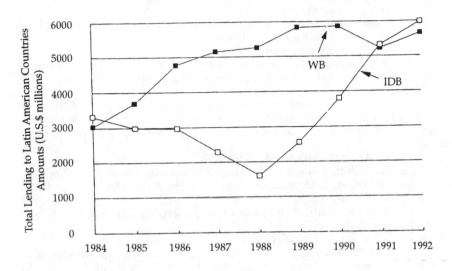

*Source:* IDB, "President's Report to the Board," 1992.

relied increasingly on its return flows and its own borrowings for its lending program.

The Bank's influence in the region was restored after the Seventh Replenishment. Since 1991 it has regained its historical role as the major source of multilateral funding to BMCs (see Figure 3.1). Against this backdrop, the Eighth Replenishment in 1994 took the overall capital base over $100 billion, and it has given the Bank a more difficult task than did large-scale dam construction in the 1970s or providing large-scale financial support in the early 1990s. These issues are discussed in the following chapters.

## Notes

1. The World Bank Charter provided that funds be used "only for the purposes for which the loan was granted" (see World Bank 1989).

2. Global loans have also been granted for a program of multiple works that are similar in nature but physically independent of one another. The executing agency here may be a DFI or any other government agency.

3. The IDB has followed the findings of the 1989 *World Development Report*, which argued that subsidized and directed credit had damaged domestic financial systems.

4. Adjustment lending is also called "fast disbursing" or "policy based," each term emphasizing a different aspect.

5. See Chapter 4.

6. The evolution of shareholdings is presented in Table 2.1.

7. This point is taken up in Chapter 5.

8. Some nonregional members voiced their concern over the lack of loans to Nicaragua (see Rudengren 1995).

9. See Chapter 5 for arrears policy.

10. Fred Bergsten, then assistant secretary at the U.S. Treasury, pushed vigorously to see both a low-income target and a cap on borrowings from Group A countries.

11. The 1982 U.S. Treasury report on the MDBs recommended that countries such as these be considered candidates for "graduation," in other words, they would be ineligible for further loans (U.S. Treasury, *U.S. Participation*, 1982).

12. See Antonio Ortiz Mena (1979).

13. See Griffith-Jones et al. (1994) and country studies in this volume.

14. Pari passu, or counterpart funds, are the funds that the borrowers must commit to each project.

15. Group A countries also have a split personality dilemma in that they are also contributors to the FSO.

16. See Arturo O'Connell (1989).

17. A systematic country focus to identify and track the development impact of projects was not introduced at the time but is now in process due to the findings and recommendations of the TAPOMA 1993 report.

18. The latest capital increase at the AsDB was agreed in 1994 with a paid-in share of 2 percent. See Kappagoda (1995).

# 4

# BORROWING COUNTRY
# EXPERIENCE

## Country Studies

This chapter will describe the experiences of three Latin American countries to illustrate the contrasting approaches of the IDB and the World Bank and to show the Bank's response to problems in individual countries. Much of the information in this chapter draws on research carried out by Ennio Rodriguez in Costa Rica and by Gonzalo Chavez in Bolivia.

In each of the three countries—Costa Rica, Bolivia, and Argentina—the IDB and the World Bank concentrated on different sectors from the beginning. In all three countries, the IDB historically contributed more resources than the World Bank. Argentina is the only country among the high-income countries (Group A) with a larger program linked to the IDB than to the World Bank. Bolivia, among the low-income countries (Group D), holds some of the lowest social indicators in the region. In contrast, Costa Rica (Group C) is among the middle-income countries and reflects the least inequality in the Latin American and Caribbean region.

IDB lending to Costa Rica and Bolivia has been double the lending by the World Bank. This highlights the small-country focus of the regional bank. In all three countries, including Argentina, the IDB was historically an important provider of funds for public sector investment programs.

The IDB played a compensatory role when the debt crisis emphasized Latin America's liquidity problem. In contrast, the World Bank put a brake on commitments and disbursements. When the Baker Plan led to an upswing in policy-based lending from the World Bank, the IDB did not change its practices. It joined the debt strategy in a more active capacity after its mandate from the Seventh Replenishment.

Following the regionwide trend in all three cases since then, the IDB has become the single most important provider of funds, although it may have been overshadowed in the country dialogue—a trend that is reversing as the macroeconomic adjustment process matures.

The IDB entered into policy loans through its expertise in sector work. It relied on programs beyond its control for the existence of an appropriate macro framework, although it still determined the impact on sector reform. Overall, an atmosphere of harmonious coexistence has prevailed with the World Bank in all three countries, although this was not true in all circumstances. Within this pattern of harmony, differentiation was sought at either subsectoral or institutional levels.

The thrust of the dialogue has remained mainly sector driven. Greater emphasis has developed on public sector management and on crosscutting issues, such as environmental management, labor training, and women in development (WID).

### Costa Rica

*Development strategy and challenges.*  Costa Rica is an established and stable democracy with a small economy highly dependent on trade. During the postwar period Costa Rica followed a growth strategy based on export diversification and import substitution (as did many developing countries). After joining the Central American Common Market (CACM), Costa Rica's strategy of export diversification consisted of selling industrial goods to the CACM and agricultural commodities to third markets.

The growth strategy during three decades was successful in transforming a low-income rural society into a middle-income, increasingly urbanized country. The fruits of growth were widely shared with the poorest peoples in the region, and this mirrored the largely inclusive political system.

The second oil shock of the 1970s hit the CACM economies hard; the downturn in international trade was not compensated for by an increase in regional trade. However, adjustment was postponed because of virtually unlimited access to commercial bank credit to finance fiscal and trade deficits. The crisis in Costa Rica exploded in August 1981, predating by a year the regionwide debt and payments crisis. Disposable per capita income decreased by 10 percent during 1982, real wages declined by 30 percent, and unemployment doubled.

A stabilization program was successfully implemented, and the external debt renegotiated in 1982. Export promotion to Third World markets became the new engine of growth, and overvaluation of the currency was avoided. An Export Ministry was created (later the Foreign Trade Ministry), and import and export bureaucratic procedures were simplified. Other reforms included the strengthening of private banks, divestiture of public enterprises, and, in general, greater reliance on the private sector.

The response of the private sector was impressive in terms of investment and export diversification. Nontraditional exports grew from 38 percent of total exports in 1985 to 55 percent in 1990. Market access was helped by the Caribbean Basin Initiative (CBI).

Successful adjustment allowed support from multilateral and bilateral institutions and strengthened Costa Rica's position vis-à-vis the commercial banks. After Costa Rica defaulted to commercial banks and some bilateral donors in the 1986–1990 period, servicing of commercial bank debt was adjusted to maintain positive net transfers and to allow growth and macroeconomic stability.

*The role of the IDB and other external agents in the country's financing.* The IDB has played a greater role than the World Bank in lending to Costa Rica. In the past two decades the two banks have lent a total of $2 billion, of which 70 percent came from the IDB.[1] At the beginning of the 1970s the World Bank played a greater role in Costa Rica than the IDB, but it gradually withdrew, reaching an all-time low during the worst years of the crisis (1982–1984). The World Bank stepped up its lending once structural adjustment was in place. In contrast, the IDB played a vital compensatory role from the onset of the crisis. Not only did the Bank maintain the level of commitments, but it agreed to fast disbursement for existing projects, thereby contributing badly needed hard currency while debt rescheduling took place.

However, the main supplier of funds in 1982–1984 was not the IDB but the United States Agency for International Development (USAID). USAID utilized its Economic Support Fund (ESF) to support stabilization efforts before the IMF and other institutions could move. During the worst crisis years, USAID commitments ($435 million) were double the funds authorized by the IDB and World Bank together ($221 million). Structural adjustment negotiations with USAID also preceded those with other multilateral institutions. The prominent U.S. role was due to Costa Rica's position as an "oasis of democracy" in a region torn by civil strife (particularly in Nicaragua and El Salvador).

The IDB's lending activities can be divided into two periods. The first (to 1990) was based on project lending, while in the 1990s the Bank moved into adjustment lending, first in cofinancing with the World Bank and then on its own. The blend between soft and ordinary capital loans from the IDB has changed since the 1970s. Soft-window oper-

ations represented 92 percent from 1970 to 1972 and declined thereafter, dropping to zero during 1985–1987. As a member of Group C,
Costa Rica can only borrow in its local currency from the FSO.

There are also two clear phases in the lending activities of the
World Bank. The turning point was in 1985 when lending was halted
and then resumed specifically for adjustment and balance-of-payments support. During the second half of the 1980s, the Bretton Woods
institutions became central in the management of the debt crisis.
Conditions established under the IMF programs and SALs complemented each other, and, although some disagreement did emerge
(such as over the exchange rate), in general close coordination between
the IMF and World Bank teams prevented disagreement and reduced
any attempts by governments to play one institution against the other.
The IDB was brought into the framework of adjustment through discussions on the level of disbursements required to close the financial
gap.

Thanks to its geopolitical importance to the United States and the
small amounts of debt involved, Costa Rica was allowed not only to
accumulate large arrears with commercial banks but also to negotiate
a very favorable debt-reduction package under the Brady initiative.
The debt reduction (measured as a percentage of outstanding debt
owed to commercial banks) was twice that obtained by Mexico and
Argentina. In Costa Rica's Brady agreement, the main instrument was
a buyback scheme at sixteen cents to the dollar. The remainder of the
debt, including part of the arrears, was converted into long-term
bonds. The response from the commercial banks surpassed expectations. To finance the agreement, $225 million was needed: more than
$100 million came from World Bank and IMF loans and the remainder
from bilateral sources (including Japan, Taiwan, the United States, and
Canada) as well as from reserves. The IDB was not involved in the
commercial debt-rescheduling exercise. The agreement did not reduce
actual debt service (current payments are similar to those of preceding
years), but because Costa Rica is not accumulating interest arrears to
commercial banks, expectations have improved. As a result of this
rescheduling exercise, the debt profile resembles that of other small
countries in which total debt is largely owed to bilateral and multilateral official creditors.

After 1985 the World Bank and the IDB restored their traditional
lending levels. However, net transfers from the World Bank remained
negative (1982–1989) and became negative from the IDB (1988–1989).
Net transfers from the IMF were also negative (1985–1989). The
increase in multilateral debt associated with the Brady Plan could
worsen these figures further. Bilateral sources have declined and are
likely to continue to decline because the geopolitical importance of
Central America has faded with the end of the Cold War.

*The IDB's role in Costa Rica's development strategy.* The three Costa Rican sectors that received the most funds from the two banks were energy, agriculture, and transportation, considered the most important by the Costa Rican government in the 1970s. The sector with the largest share of external funding was energy (39 percent), of which almost all came from the IDB. Agriculture was a distant second for funds from the banks (17 percent), and again the largest contribution came from the IDB (84 percent). Transportation was the third largest (16 percent of total loans), and in this case the World Bank was the largest lender (56 percent).

To some extent, energy projects received the most funds because of the excellent capacity of staff in this sector for planning and project execution. During the energy crises of the 1970s, energy programs became the highest priority for development banks. These investments allowed energy supply to keep pace with the demand fueled by demographic growth, rapid urbanization, and industrialization.

During the 1970s, improvement of the rural sector was a top priority as a means to attack poverty and reduce rural-urban migration flows. It was a period of active state intervention to promote growth and investment with sector-targeted instruments and with the backing and financial support of the development banks. Agriculture had higher costs because of import substitution, but these were balanced through subsidized interest rates and improvements in transportation infrastructure. Investment in transportation was also a means to improve the living conditions of the rural poor. Energy program investments included a rural electrification program. Other priority sectors of the decade were education and health, but they relied mostly on fiscal revenues. In short, the development priorities relied on an ambitious public sector investment program supported by the development banks.

During the years of easy private credit (1976–1981), borrowing from the multilateral banks did not decline accordingly; in fact, borrowing from the IDB increased. Public investment in transportation and energy continued to rely on multilateral loans, which had grace and repayment periods best suited to the projects. In the 1980s, the IDB continued lending to agriculture. Subsidies to the end-users were withdrawn, with the exception of a large irrigation project, which was continued without producers bearing total water costs. Other areas of IDB specialization have been the social sectors: the environment (73 percent of multilateral lending from the IDB); education (88 percent); and urban development (100 percent).

After the Seventh Replenishment, the IDB participated more intensely in adjustment operations. It joined the World Bank in a loan to the education sector (World Bank $23 million, IDB $28 million) and a loan for health services (World Bank $50 million, IDB $100 million).

The IDB also cofinanced the SAL III (World Bank $100 million, IDB $100 million). In these operations there is a subsectoral institutional specialization.

The investment sector loan (ISL) is not cofinanced, but it carries an agreement with the IMF as a precondition, which makes it akin to the SAL in terms of cross-conditionality. The ISL is a prerequisite for U.S. bilateral debt forgiveness within the EAI and for the Multilateral Investment Fund (MIF) administered by the IDB. As can be seen, the IDB is assuming a critical role in the administration of the EAI and is participating actively in the bilateral relationship between the United States and the Latin American and Caribbean countries.

*Project experience.*   Relations between the Costa Rican government and the development banks were cordial in project lending; the development banks were seen as supporting the long-term public investment priorities. Project execution was also satisfactory, although major delays took place due to the need to get loans ratified by the Costa Rican Congress.

Few recent project evaluations are available, but the 1970s water and sewerage project in five cities has taught some lessons. The system in San José was assessed as inadequate, for the subsequent results showed that the majority of potential users chose to remain in the old system, avoiding the higher cost of the new one. As a result, only half of the sewer connections were in use when the ex post facto evaluation was carried out. Operation and maintenance of the sewer system were not completely satisfactory. Moreover, the executing agency had not fulfilled its commitment to charge full price to cover maintenance, operation, and amortization costs.

The Arenal hydroelectric project, whose last three generating units entered into operation in the 1980s, was successfully completed in terms of physical works, plant, and machinery. However, the execution period exceeded projections by approximately two years, and the final cost of the project was twice the original estimate. This project required the resettlement of two existing communities, Tronadora and Arenal. Perhaps the most salient socioeconomic aspect of the project was the orderly, efficient, and socially responsible manner in which the executing agency (Instituto Costariccence de Electricidad, ICE) carried out resettlement of both communities. The new settlements not only provided improved conditions but also offered technical assistance and social services. The implementation of the project produced a change in the land tenure system. Before the project, the land had been concentrated in large holdings owned by a few absentee landlords who hired local laborers. After resettlement, most laborers owned a plot and derived their livelihood from small-scale farming activities.

*The future.* Concern for the environment is the most significant change in recent IDB lending. Environmental impact has been incorporated as part of project feasibility studies. Technical cooperation is strengthening local capabilities to enforce environmental regulations. Specific environmental projects, as well as postgraduate programs, are being promoted to evaluate environmental impact and the economics of natural resources.

The IDB is expected to be the main external source of finance for the public investment program, representing 25 to 33 percent of the total investment. The Central American Bank for Economic Integration is expected to play a larger role than the World Bank (see Table 4.1).

Table 4.1    **Programmed Public Investments by Funding Agency, Costa Rica: 1993–1995 (in millions of colones)**

|  | 1993 | | 1994 | | 1995 | |
| --- | --- | --- | --- | --- | --- | --- |
|  | Amount | % | Amount | % | Amount | % |
| Inter-American Development Bank | 26,001.3 | 30.5 | 24,320.0 | 32.7 | 8,476.5 | 21.2 |
| Central American Bank for Economic Integration | 4,701.4 | 5.5 | 4,602.2 | 6.2 | 1,974.3 | 5.0 |
| World Bank | 2,888.3 | 3.4 | 2,560.9 | 3.4 | 2,375.5 | 5.9 |
| Others | 51,713.0 | 60.6 | 42,959.5 | 57.7 | 27,165.6 | 67.9 |
| Total | 85,304.0 | 100.0 | 74,442.6 | 100.0 | 39,991.9 | 100.0 |

*Source:* Various documents of the Ministerio de Planificación y Política Económica, Costa Rica (Ministry of Economic Policy and Planning).

President Iglesias first proposed that Costa Rica's response to social needs be taken as an example in the new social reform strategy of the Bank and be used as a testing ground for new policies. But the outgoing administration of Costa Rica considered that direct measures of poverty alleviation for vulnerable groups should continue to be financed from the budget, as has been the practice, to avoid a further burden on external indebtedness. Indebtedness to multilateral and bilateral sources is a cause for considerable concern. The IDB's exposure in Costa Rica is already quite high at 41 percent of total multilateral debt.

*Bolivia*

*The development strategy.* Bolivian economic growth has been elusive. Until the mid-1980s, the development strategy was based on heavy state intervention. The model of state capitalism that emerged in the

1950s reached its peak in the 1970s. Investment, mainly concentrated in the public sector, reached 20 percent of GDP. In 1970 and 1975 the economy registered unprecedented growth rates of 5 percent and 7 percent respectively, with one-digit inflation rates. But from that point on signs of fatigue surfaced. Fiscal and inflationary problems became evident, and by 1977 a turning point was reached. The subsequent contraction of international credit, the collapse in the price of tin (Bolivia's main commodity), and Argentina's arrears on gas purchases (Bolivia's second most important export earner) led to an economic collapse that lasted from 1982 to 1985.

By August 1985, Bolivia was in chaos. The annual inflation rate came close to 24,000 percent; the public deficit was over 30 percent of GDP; the investment rate barely reached 9 percent; and foreign debt was equivalent to GDP. A stabilization and adjustment program, known as the New Economic Policy (NEP), was implemented in 1985. The main pillars of the program were (1) an anti-inflationary shock (exchange rate unification and a return to full convertibility, which led to a 93 percent devaluation); (2) full internal and external market liberalization; and (3) severe fiscal and monetary adjustment, which included a debt moratorium and tax reform. Layoffs in the public sector were massive. For example, the state mining enterprise reduced its workforce from thirty thousand to seven thousand.

Since then Bolivia has moved from state capitalism to a privatized economy. Initially the most noticeable result of the program was the substantial fall in inflation. After 1987, the rate of inflation stabilized at around 15 percent a year. Recovery of growth was modest until 1992. In 1992 the economy grew at 4 percent, which brought about the first real per capita growth rate since 1977. Exports, however, declined.

The rate of investment was in a steady downswing. It picked up in 1991, reaching a modest 13 percent of GDP. The level of unemployment and quasi employment is still high, estimated at 18 percent. Crisis and subsequent adjustment had a severe impact on per capita income levels, but social indicators did not deteriorate, as can be seen in Table 4.2. The IDB contributed to this performance with the implementation of an emergency social fund. Despite these improvements social conditions in Bolivia remain among the worst in Latin America.

*Relationship of the IDB with other donors.*  Bolivia receives a large volume of financial aid. An amount equivalent to one-fifth of the GDP flows into the country in the form of loans and grants. Bolivia is second after Ecuador in Group D (the low-income countries) in total loans received from the IDB since 1970.

At the same time, the IDB has been the most important provider of funds to the Bolivian economy. From 1970 to 1990 it doubled the

Table 4.2   Social and Demographic Indicators, Bolivia

| | 1976 (%) | 1988 (%) | Latin America[a] 1990 (%) |
|---|---|---|---|
| Annual rate of population growth | 2.05 | 2.03 | 2.5 |
| Urban | 3.84 | 4.10 | |
| Rural | 1.14 | −0.01 | |
| Urban population as a percent of total population | 42.0 | 58.0 | 72.0 |
| Rural population as a percent of total population | 58.0 | 42.0 | 28.0 |
| Life expectancy (years) | 51.0 | 59.0 | 67.0 |
| Men | — | 51.1 | |
| Women | — | 60.7 | |
| General mortality (in thousands) | 18.1 | 10.58 | 8.0 |
| Fertility (children per woman) total | 6.5 | 5.0 | 3.4 |
| Urban | 5.2 | 4.0 | |
| Rural | 7.5 | 6.5 | |
| Infant mortality (in thousands) | 151 | 102 | 70 |
| Malnutrition | | | |
| Chronic | — | 38.3 | |
| Severe | — | 2.5 | |
| Urban | — | 45.0 | |
| Rural | — | 31.5 | |
| Total national access to water services | 39.0 | 60.0 | 77.0 |
| Urban | — | 89.3 | 88.0 |
| Rural | — | 30.5 | 66.0 |
| Population in housing without basic services | 52.0 | 39.0 | 35.0 |
| Urban | 50.0 | 39.0 | 35.0 |
| Rural | 53.0 | 40.0 | |
| Total illiteracy | 37.0 | 18.9 | 16.0 |
| Rural illiteracy | 63.0 | 31.1 | |
| Men | — | 19.1 | |
| Women | — | 42.0 | |
| Population in poverty | 74.0 | 64.0 | 61.8 |
| Urban | 62.0 | 56.0 | |
| Rural | 82.0 | 73.0 | |

*Source:* National Institute of Statistics (CNPV 1976, ENPV 1988); UNDP 1990.
*Notes:* a. Includes the Caribbean countries.

amount of commitments from the World Bank. When the crisis broke out (in 1982), the World Bank froze its commitments to Bolivia. As described in the other case studies, the IDB did not. Disbursements were doubled. Between 1982 and 1986 Bolivia's net transfers to the World Bank amounted to U.S. $45 million and were partially compensated for by IDA transfers of U.S. $16 million. The IDB, in contrast, provided a total of U.S. $288 million in the same period. In 1983 the IDB provided emergency assistance to cope with floods and droughts.

With the NEP underway, commitments from the IDB doubled, and Bolivia received more then a quarter of all the loans to Group D.

Although the World Bank stepped up its lending via policy-based operations to accompany the reform program, the volume of loans from the IDB still remained ahead. Sixty percent of total multilateral lending during the reform process was from the IDB, and it has contributed between 16 and 18 percent of the public investment program.

Over the twenty-year period, half of these loans were made from ordinary capital resources, and the other half were concessional. There were, however, variations over time. Concessional resources made up more than 80 percent of the lending program from 1976 to 1978. Thereafter, with the drying up of the FSO, they declined significantly, and at the onset of the reform program the IDB was almost devoid of concessional loans. They have increased since then and are expected to make up the total future lending program (IDB, *Bolivia: Country Programming Paper*, 1993).

*Role of the Bank in Bolivia.*    The role of the Bank in Bolivia has three periods that correspond to the country's changing development strategies: the first was during the phase of state capitalism; the second corresponds to the launching of the NEP; and the third is during the present phase, in which adjustment continues at a steady but more gradual pace.

The IDB and the World Bank followed complementary patterns during the period of state capitalism. The division of labor showed a slight variation from the regional pattern of the World Bank being involved mainly in transportation and the IDB in energy programs. Before the 1973 oil price hike, the IDB was dedicated to road building; subsequently it concentrated in building gas exports to Argentina. The World Bank focused mainly on developing mining resources. Transportation was a distant second, and operations concentrated on railroad development. Social sectors received negligible attention from the World Bank until the NEP.

The pattern altered after the NEP. The World Bank, together with the IMF, took the lead in the policy reform process, both in funding and policy design. At the same time, the World Bank started operations in social sectors. Nevertheless, the IDB remained the main supplier of funds. The policy dialogue was led by the IMF and the World Bank with which the country signed the Policy Framework Paper. Between 1988 and 1992, four ESAF agreements with the IMF were signed. Loans from the World Bank were mainly policy-based IDA loans. In contrast, the lack of sufficient concessional funds during the Seventh Replenishment meant that IDB operations were drawn mainly from ordinary capital resources.

As in other countries, after the IDB gained a role in the adjustment process with the Seventh Replenishment, coordination between both banks became more deliberate and active. The pattern has varied from joint operations to taking turns at giving assistance depending on the issues. The World Bank initiated a project for forestry and land titling that built on previous technical assistance provided by the IDB. There is a joint education reform program and a joint municipal development project to improve public administration, privatization, and fiscal management of local governments. Building on the financial sector adjustment loans of the World Bank, the banks are cofinancing a financial sector reform and investment sector loan to improve resource allocation efficiency of the financial sector and capital markets, to streamline the performance of public sector enterprises, and to liberalize private sector investment regulations. In turn, IDA's Regulatory Reform and Capitalization Program has been conceived as a second stage to the ISL/structural adjustment credit.

Both banks are dedicated to enhancing tax collection, to building Bolivia's export capacity in agriculture and mining, and to supporting the development of infrastructure for the delivery of exports. The IDB is carrying out a technical cooperation program to restructure the customs service and gives a high priority to the social sectors in the country's social action plan.

*Project experience.*    The Bank's presence in Bolivia contributed significantly to improvements in social conditions and physical infrastructure. There are few audited ex post facto evaluations of loans, but the ones available indicate that in social sectors physical goals have generally been achieved, albeit with delays. The problem lies in the practice of setting unrealistic deadlines. The IDB has relied on a four-year implementation period, which can seldom be executed. Flexible periods of disbursements have not been applied, leading to expected (and avoidable) delays.

The major problems are the administrative and accounting weaknesses of executing units. Delays in project implementation have occurred mainly in the transportation and energy sectors. Transportation projects have consistently suffered delays. There have been some faulty project designs, but problems were mainly caused by procurement and bidding requirements and by difficulties in the coordination of external financing. The average rate of loans undisbursed for all multilateral and bilateral donors stands at a little below 30 percent. The IDB has been slightly above average. In 1992 the IDB managed an improvement in its loan portfolio, and disbursements reached projected levels. Undisbursed balances on fully executed operations up to $64 million were canceled; the amount of $6 million was granted under the revolving Project Preparation Facility, and a preinvestment multisector loan was approved.

*The future.*   Bolivia's adjustment has been slow and painful and still requires multilateral support and concessional funding. The government relies on grants and concessional borrowing for financing its deficit on external current accounts. The ratio of public external debt to GDP has been reduced from 87 percent in 1987 to 59 percent in 1994, a level still dangerously high. The ratio of overall debt service to exports ratio has also improved from 49 percent to 33 percent. Overall payment capacity may gradually expand, but it is fragile, being sensitive to metal prices and to gas demand from neighboring countries, despite all attempts at export diversification.

The share of IDB loans in Bolivia's total debt has increased from 24 percent in 1990 to an estimated 29 percent in 1992; the Bank is the most exposed of all creditors. Nonetheless, the Bank expects to remain the major source of external finance for Bolivia and to provide only concessional loans, with priority to social sectors and the expansion of export capacity. Yet the assumption of new debt will increase exposure further, and, if export growth does not materialize as expected, Bolivia's payment problems will increase the risk of the Bank.

## Argentina

*Development strategy and main challenges.*   Postwar Argentina has usually been depicted as the paradigm of an inward-oriented and highly regulated economy, which has historically suffered from sluggish growth. Income inequalities remain among the smallest in Latin America, even after the marked deterioration in living standards during the 1980s. Import substitution was accompanied by mounting macroeconomic disequilibria aggravated by the 1982 debt crisis. Consumer prices rose by an annual average of 450 percent in the decade leading to 1990. Over the same ten years, income per capita fell by more than 20 percent, and investment slumped from 20 percent to 7 percent of GDP.

Structural reform began in 1987, partly at the behest of the World Bank. Since 1990 reform has accelerated, transforming a highly regulated state-centered economy into an open, market-oriented one. The centerpiece of the reform has been the public sector. The primary deficit (net of interest payments) moved into a 4 percent surplus by mid-1991. Privatization has trimmed the government's debt by approximately $12 billion through debt-equity swaps and has brought in receipts of nearly $7 billion.

In April 1991 the Convertibility Act made the peso fully convertible at a fixed rate to the dollar; by law the monetary base was backed by gold and foreign reserves. The act required the Central Bank to act as a currency board; changes to the exchange rate now required congressional approval. The act also banned indexation of wages. In March 1991 the IMF provided an EFF of $3 billion, mostly earmarked for Brady Plan enhancements, and the remainder barely covered repayments on past drawings. A year later Argentina reached a Brady Plan agreement. This produced a debt reduction equivalent of about $9 billion out of a total debt of $58 billion.

Growth in Argentina reached an average of 7 percent in 1991–1993 after experiencing negative rates in 1988–1989 and being almost nil in 1990. Heavy external inflows ($5 billion in 1991 and $9 billion in 1992) went mostly into the debt conversion/privatization program and the stock market.

Over the past decade public investment contracted from 12 percent to less then 2.5 percent of GDP. This dive led to a deterioration of infrastructure and the provision of social services. Health standards fell, reflected in the reemergence of tuberculosis, malaria, and cholera. The provision of public services may deteriorate further, given the transfer of responsibility to weak provincial and municipal governments.

*The role of the IDB and other external agents in Argentina.*    The IDB maintained a presence in Argentina throughout the last two decades, even when there was easy access to private markets, as described in the other case studies. Commitments increased at a steady pace, and transfers from the IDB remained positive. In contrast, transfers from the World Bank became negative by the second half of the 1970s.

The Baker Plan marked a temporary break with precedent as the World Bank began to play a more important role in Argentina's funding and the IDB declined markedly. From 1970 to 1985 the World Bank approved operations for $1.5 billion (less than half of the IDB). In the second half of the 1980s, World Bank commitments rose to $3 billion, more than double the IDB commitments in the same period. Between 1985 and 1990, loan approvals from the IDB averaged $230 million a year. No new loans were approved in 1987[2] and 1990, partly because of the Bank's internal crisis and partly because of budgetary constraints placed on pari passu funding.

The shift also had an impact on net transfers. During the second half of the 1980s, Argentina received a positive net transfer from the World Bank but there were fluctuating negative transfers from the IDB and the IMF. The shift was also reflected in their relative exposure: the IDB's share in total external debt increased from 2.6 percent in 1985 to 4.1 percent in 1991, and the World Bank's share increased from 1.4 percent to 4.4 percent.

During the mid-1980s the World Bank temporarily became a key participant both in the determination of the flow of funds and in the monitoring of adjustment. The World Bank's heavy involvement in Argentina led to a controversy between the IMF and the World Bank over how much stabilization was required before structural adjustment took place. The World Bank—under pressure from the U.S. Treasury—flouted established procedures and sidestepped the IMF in granting its policy-based lending when Argentina was piling up arrears in its interest payments to the commercial banks.

The conflicting nature of these World Bank loans to Argentina brought home the risk of competition between financial agents (Tussie and Botzman 1990). Initially Argentina might have benefited by playing one institution against the other but this situation was a disadvantage when funding decisions were linked. The experience led to changed attitudes toward dealing with the MDBs. Argentina has applied the lesson not only to World Bank–IMF relations but also to bringing the World Bank and the IDB to the same table. Since 1991 the IDB has regained its leading role in the provision of funds. Its country strategy takes into account the medium-term program with the World Bank.

*The IDB and World Bank in sectoral development.*   The few operations financed by the World Bank in the early 1970s were almost entirely in the transportation sector; about 40 percent of the IDB's went into energy programs. The IDB also undertook credit operations for industry and agriculture through development finance institutions.

This de facto division of labor vanished at the end of the 1970s with the coordinated financing of the massive hydroelectric projects. Both banks became heavily involved in this sector from this time on. When joint financing for the Yacyreta Dam was approved in 1979, most of both banks' lending to Argentina was dedicated to energy projects. The Paraguayan-Argentine hydroelectric station received $210 million from each bank in 1979. The sum was the largest single loan in the IDB's history.

Argentina's public sector portfolio was confined to a few projects and was heavily concentrated in the energy sector initially to overcome a perceived bottleneck in the region as a whole and in Argentina in particular. The Energy Secretariat was active in its search for coordinated external finance. It was almost the sole agency (with the Ministry of Agriculture) that retained well-trained staff, some institutional initiative, and policy continuity, which allowed it to generate a flow of projects. Hydroelectric projects were also actively encouraged at the time by the field office.

An outstanding feature of the IDB's lending activity in Argentina has been the amount of direct funding provided to the private sector: $300 million or about 5 percent of the lending program. In contrast to the small loans of the 1960s, during the 1970s and 1980s the sums involved in individual operations were large and favored the local conglomerates, which were expanding rapidly in the production of intermediary goods. Also in contrast to earlier loans, government guarantees were provided.

The IDB moved more quickly on loans to private firms than those to the public sector. But all loans to private firms faced servicing problems when the debt crisis broke out, with the exception of the one to the Siderca steel mill, which was granted in 1985 after the debt crisis.

IDB-financed projects also played a major role in the development of the rural water sector, in the expansion of water and sewerage services in metropolitan Buenos Aires, and in the provision of services as part of public housing schemes. Following the trend for the region as a whole, the IDB was the main source of external finance for investment in water provision. Starting in 1966, the IDB granted five loans for the provision of potable water to rural communities. During 1970–1990, total commitments by the IDB for sanitation amounted to $440 million, about 10 percent of the Bank's lending program. The World Bank made loans to this sector beginning only in the mid-1980s.

*Project experience.* The Yacyreta dam project has troubled both banks' relations with Argentina despite their good working relationship with each other in the sector. There is consensus today that the dam was an oversized undertaking with an inadequate feasibility study. Finance for approximately U.S. $1.2 billion was put together in 1979 with contributions from the Argentine Finance Ministry, the World Bank, the IDB, the U.S. Ex-Im Bank, and a consortium of commercial banks led by Morgan Guaranty. The project took on a life of its own in a maze of vested interests. Original assessments were underestimated; it turned out to be an expensive proposition not only in terms of construction costs but also for the unit price of energy that it yielded. Suspicions were raised over bidding awards. Before site-preparation work began, the geography and soil conditions of the dam site on the Paraguayan border were found unsuitable. The 1979 IDB and World Bank loan disbursements were delayed. There was an eight-year delay in the commissioning of the first unit and additional engineering and administrative expenditures. By the time the civilian government was elected in 1983, indebtedness and inflation had eroded public finances. World Bank and IDB terms were renegotiated in 1983 when it became clear that the project would be more costly to close down than to continue. So, despite the charges of corruption, new loans were approved at both banks. Construction is going ahead, albeit with lower dam elevation and turbines spaced out over a longer time period. These alterations will allow the dam to operate sooner and accelerate the expected flow of internal resources. But new disagreements over the price paid for land appropriated from communities on the Paraguayan side of the border may lead to further delays.

However, prior to the Yacyreta dam, the IDB financed the Salto Grande Project, where the ex post facto evaluation is generally positive. Dam construction commenced in April 1974, and power generation was initiated in May 1979. Salto Grande stands out as one of the few large hydroelectric development projects in the world where environmental effects were carefully investigated and anticipated. The town of Federación was rebuilt on a new site with the residents' participation; the new town is well planned. The program was institutionally and operationally more successful than anticipated. The Salto Grande's engineering program received the Ingersoll-Rand award for technical and organizational excellence, and the emphasis on environmental protection was recognized as exemplary for the world by the United Nations Environmental Programme.

*Adjustment lending under the Seventh Replenishment.* Argentina's financial needs in the early 1990s led to a concentration on fast-disbursing loans that required World Bank participation. The IDB's program initially had to lean heavily on the existing World Bank pipeline. The reconciliation of objectives between both banks does not seem to have posed major problems. At both headquarters and at the country level, productive working relationships existed to link the institutions. As a result, both IFIs worked together to establish the volume and direction of their lending program. The cooperation that started as a training relationship has now evolved into coordination at a subsectoral and institutional level.

Lending from the IDB has picked up at an accelerated pace since 1991, a year after the Seventh Replenishment guidelines were in place, but when the reform program was already under way. Policy loans were given immediate priority until the end of 1992. In 1991 approvals reached $879 million with 60 percent directed to policy reform. In 1992 and 1993 Argentina received the largest volume of loan commitments from the IDB, totaling over a billion dollars each year. In 1992 practically 100 percent were policy-based, but in 1993 100 percent were investment loans.

The centerpiece of the 1991 program was Argentina's fiscal improvement (see Figure 4.1). As a cofinancing measure, each bank authorized $325 million for a fast-disbursing public sector reform loan (PSRL), U.S. $100 million for policy reform and investment in water supply and sewerage, and $200 million for institutional reform and investment in provincial governments.

**Figure 4.1    IDB's Adjustment Lending in Argentina**

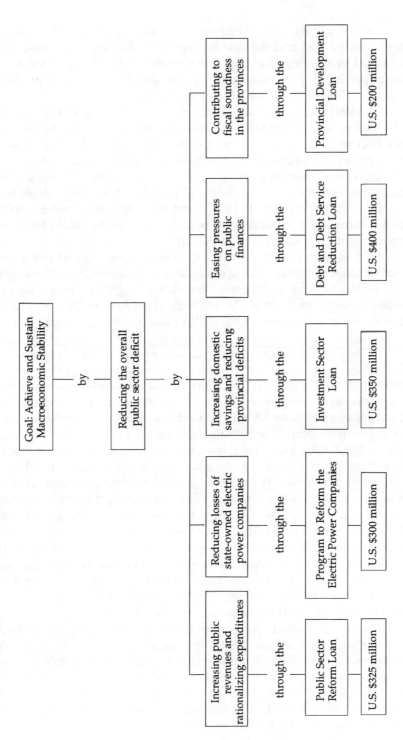

The 1991 PSRL was among the first adjustment operations under-taken by the IDB and the first in Argentina. IDB representatives par-ticipated in all World Bank missions related to this loan, and the mis-sions produced joint aide memoirs. In addition, the IDB provided resources for consultants and loan preparation.

The 1991 jointly financed loan for the water and sewerage utilities ($70 million equivalent from the ordinary capital and $30 million from the FSO in local currency) was devised by both banks. Both institu-tions have coordinated project preparation and worked together on a common understanding on project objectives, the financing plan, major project components, and conditionality. The World Bank built on the IDB's expertise in the field, and the IDB is concerned with the policy component. A condition of effectiveness at the World Bank was approval of the parallel loan at the IDB.

With respect to privatization, the banks have worked out a divi-sion of labor whereby each takes charge of different public enterpris-es. The World Bank authorized a fast-disbursing $300 million loan for railroads and oilfields, and the IDB authorized $165 million for provin-cial electric utilities and a $300 million loan for the metropolitan elec-tric utility.

An investment sector loan (ISL) was approved in 1992 to reform legislation to improve the climate for private sector investment. In 1992 the IDB also provided support for the Brady Plan by means of a debt and debt-service reduction loan of $400 million (to finance par bond collaterals), to be added to up to $244 million of set asides includ-ed in previous loans. The IDB also waived the negative pledge restric-tion in the Bank's loan and guarantee agreements with Argentina up to $3.7 billion to allow the government to pledge collateral for the dis-count and par bonds. The conclusion of the debt agreement required total enhancements of about $3.6 billion, including the down payment on interest arrears. The IDB provided $644 million, the World Bank $750 million, the IMF $1,040 million, and Japan's Ex-Im Bank $800 mil-lion. Argentina provided financing to close the difference. IDB, World Bank, and IMF funds were disbursed simultaneously after the debt agreement was formally subscribed to by the private banks and the government. The loan has no specific policy conditionality beyond maintaining the fiscal framework of the overall program.

The DDSR loan contributed to the restructuring of all medium- and long-term commercial debt, amounting to about $20.9 billion (half of Argentina's public and publicly guaranteed debt) and approximate-ly $8.3 billion on past due interest. The reduction was applied only to the principal outstanding while interest arrears were settled by a par-tial down payment of $700 million and an exchange of the remainder for par bonds bearing market interest rates.

Despite the number of loans approved by the IDB after the Seventh Replenishment, disbursements have lagged; execution posed more problems than anticipated. It is now evident that the Bank's central administration did not have the institutional and legal capacity to deliver the financial resources needed. It is also likely that Argentina made some unrealistic commitments, implicitly accepting that only partial disbursement of the overall loan would follow.

*The future.*   There are currently three levels of dialogue: (1) definition of the macro policy framework that is a precondition to substantial lending; (2) sector conditions; and (3) project-specific conditions. The first country program exercise began in 1991 with a country programming paper (CPP) produced in March 1992. Yearly programming missions continue the process.

Argentina has now exhausted the fast-disbursing resources available for policy reform, so further reforms must be supported by policy-driven investment loans. Sharply increased IDB resources are expected for social sectors. In fact, in the medium and long term the IDB hopes to shift the focus of its assistance, coinciding with national priorities of the government's medium-term strategy, to support: (1) the level, quality, and targeting of social services; and (2) investment in directly productive activities that would enhance international competitiveness. Initial social programs are policy oriented and are expected to improve institutional capabilities for the delivery of services at the provincial level. Overall, the Bank's assessment of the country's prospects is one of cautious optimism. It is also aware that decentralization of social services to the provincial and municipal levels may exacerbate the problem of delivery in the short run.

Until the Brady agreement was closed Argentina had a keen interest in fast-disbursing loans. The requirement to coordinate such operations with the World Bank left little room for new initiatives. Once the requirement was lifted, the generation of operations flowed from both sides. As part of a general drive in the region the IDB undertook a program for labor retraining to provide a line of credit for ongoing activities rather than to undertake traditional projects. The Bank offered technical assistance in view of its experience in Chile and seems also prepared to fund study trips for public officials to learn from the Chilean experience.

Argentina has taken the initiative in presenting several projects for road development and has asked for support to continue the Yacyreta project. The IDB has resisted providing more funds for civil works until the result of an ongoing loan from the World Bank is known; instead it has offered to provide assistance for the protection of the environment and for population relocation.

With regard to the Eighth Replenishment, Argentine authorities are receptive to putting social policy reform on the agenda. Moreover, investments in social sectors and social issues have been singled out as a government priority in the recent medium-term plan. Thus, the government is, in principle, not averse to initiating a social policy dialogue, but it is concerned about realistic conditionalities and the implementation of programs.

Legislative reform is by definition a slow process in a democracy where consensus must be built, as pointed out by the finance minister in the IDB's 1993 annual meeting in Hamburg. Furthermore, policy reform requires management, and management requires institutions that must be built in present-day Argentina. This is more critical for future social policy than for macroeconomic management, because ministries in charge are much weaker then the treasury. Future concerns in this area have been identified by both the Argentine government and the IDB. A preinvestment loan will allow the study of projects from the initial conceptualization to the final design, and a PPF is earmarked to follow projects from Profile II onwards. But more support in the form of technical assistance will be needed. The ability to design and implement projects at the national, provincial, and local levels is critical to build social reform.

## Notes

1. The same is not true, however, for Group C as a whole. The World Bank has lent more to Jamaica and Uruguay.
2. Except for a small one of U.S. $2.7 million.

# PART 2

## DEVELOPMENT AGENDA

# 5

# Loan Performance and Institutional Governance

This chapter describes the institutional and loan performance of the IDB. The first section of this chapter assesses the Bank's performance in lending to low-income segments of the population. This mandate is particular to the IDB, but the articulation of the objective has been vague. It is now under reformulation as concerns about poverty gain in force and substance. The sections that follow describe the project cycle and institutional organization. Lastly, the chapter describes the problems in assessing the quality of loans and the steps taken to address the problems of monitoring.

More than other regional development banks, the IDB's overall direction has been influenced by the United States' vision of development and its foreign policy priorities, which have had several changes in direction.

The IDB, alone among the multilateral banks, was created with a soft loan window as an integral part of its juridical structure. Thanks to U.S. support, the FSO was exceptionally well endowed with resources in comparison with the Asian Development Bank and the African Development Bank (Culpeper 1993). Shortly after the Bank was set up, the United States provided an additional $394 million for a concessional Social Progress Trust Fund as a part of the Alliance for Progress.

Some of the early lending activities of the 1960s were part of the strategic competitiveness of the Cold War. When these loans ran into difficulties they came under criticism for being "too soft" and unsuited to a bank. By 1970, however, the emphasis on social projects had waned, and the Bank took a more conservative approach. But it had difficulty in fulfilling one of the basic tenets for which it had been established, namely, support to local industry. An independent consulting firm, ADELATEC, attributed the difficulties in finding enough industrial projects to finance to the caution and conservatism of the IDB's evaluation procedures and its exacting requirements in making loans (Dell 1972).

These contrasting cycles clearly illustrate the challenge faced by the IDB's management in striking the right balance between careful administration and sound lending on the one hand and meeting visions of development on the other. The demands on the present president are no exception. A dedicated Latin Americanist, having served as secretary general of the Economic Commission for Latin America and the Caribbean, Enrique Iglesias brought fundamental issues to the attention of both nonborrowing and borrowing member countries and is recognized as a leading "development voice." Iglesias has given the Bank a renewed sense of mission and in 1992 was elected to a second five-year term.

Voting power at the IDB is heavily concentrated in the United States and the four major BMCs. The influence of the United States was modified as new nonborrowing members, Canada and the nonregional countries, were admitted. However, for some time the contributions of new nonborrowing member countries were mainly in the area of resource mobilization. Over time, their influence has increased, and they have a vital balancing role, able to shape and guide certain Bank policies. Through a regional development bank, smaller non-BMCs have access to borrowing countries.

Until the Eighth Replenishment, the small non-BMCs, the nonregionals plus Canada, held only 11.58 percent of the voting power, but the correlation between formal voting power and influence is not one to one. Since the Board operates by consensus, what matters more than formal voting power is the degree of effort and interest that countries put into preparing their positions and their determination to pursue particular issues.

Nonetheless, the redistribution of global financial power allowed a realignment of shares during the Eighth Replenishment in 1994. Nonregional countries doubled their voting shares from 7.1 percent to 15.9 percent and now have an additional chair. Japan, in line with its new global power, now has a chair of its own with 5 percent of voting power, up from 1.08 percent.

## Experience Under the Low-Income Goal

Latin America contains the most unequal income distribution in the world. The wealthiest fifth of the region's population earns twenty times that of the poorest fifth, compared to a ratio of about ten to one in Asia. It should be noted that these are income distribution comparisons; death by starvation is virtually unknown in the region. During the three decades, 1950 to 1980, because of relatively rapid growth before "the lost decade," social indicators improved marledly although income inequality continued to worsen. In the 1970s the perception that the benefits of growth were not trickling down inspired the World Bank approach to "growth with redistribution."

At the conclusion of discussions for the Fifth Replenishment in December 1978, the Bank's goal was to ensure that 50 percent of its lending program be allocated to benefit low-income groups. The IDB is the only multilateral development bank with such a mandate. The idea was initially introduced by the United States and drew support from Canada and various nonregional members. The Carter administration proposed a program of rural development as a means to reduce rural poverty and control the inflow of Mexicans and Central Americans across the border.

The proposal reads: "The Bank should intensify its efforts to channel resources to projects which provide benefits to the low-income groups, especially in the matter of improving the productivity and income of these groups. The Bank further should define these groups more precisely and aim at devoting one half of its lending from Bank resources during the period of the next replenishment to such projects" (IDB, *Proposal for an Increase*, 1978, 55). There was a focus on rural development with a 30–35 percent allocation of resources and on urban development with the allocation of 10–15 percent of resources. "In summary, about 50 percent of the proposed lending program would be oriented to benefitting directly the low-income groups, primarily through projects which stress the creation of productive employment" (ibid).

The sectoral targets were met at the minimum of the targeted range; that is, when the target was 20–30 percent, lending reached 20 percent rather than 30 percent. The low-income goal was more elusive. Management interpreted the goal to mean that 50 percent of the benefits of the lending program should be appropriated to low-income people; but the implementation of the mandate has been riddled with problems. Borrowers accepted the general purpose of the proposal and contributed to a methodology based on their experience. At the same time, they were reluctant to contemplate a formula that could rigidly impose preset criteria to determine priorities for the selection of projects. This was especially true in the large countries where there was no shortage of profitable projects. Thus the guidelines to put the low-income goal into practice had to allow room to accommodate other priorities (or other means to reach the end) and resulted in a modification of the original mandate.

The guidelines stipulated that the ex ante measurement of distrib-

utive impact would not be a basis for accepting or rejecting a loan proposal. The low-income goal has thus been divorced from strategic
planning, the process of loan selection, evaluation, and approval, as
well as from the allocation of resources by country and sector. In practice, this meant that the Bank could not insist on doing low-income
projects because it was not a criteria for designing a loan program.
Moreover, it should be noted that the mandate did not call for social
lending as such; it did, however, stress employment creation.

To render the mandate operational, low-income groups were identified through the cost of a minimum food basket in each country.
Low-income levels were expressed in local currencies to avoid problems of exchange rate conversion. The proposed levels were discussed
with country authorities to avoid triggering political controversies.
The definition of the low-income population and the break-off point
tended to be negotiable. Some countries, such as Paraguay, preferred a
lower cut-off point to hide politically sensitive poverty indicators; others, such as Argentina, preferred a higher cut-off point to increase the
number of low-income beneficiaries. The range was wide. For example, in Peru the poor were classified as those with a per capita annual
income of U.S. $646 (71 percent of the population) whereas the UN
Development Programme (UNDP, *Human Development Report*, 1991)
estimated U.S. $260 per capita as the dividing line for the lowest 40
percent of the households. In Mexico the low-income groups were
defined as those with an average per capita income of U.S. $1,245
while the UNDP gave an average per capita for the lowest 40 percent
of households as U.S. $450.

Bank staff developed a methodology to measure and report the
expected distribution of economic benefits.[1] Where cost-benefit analysis was used, the direct net benefits to low-income groups were calculated as a share of total net benefits in the private sector—disregarding
public sector benefits because of the difficulties involved. Where measurement of direct net benefits was not feasible, as in most social development projects, the distributive impact was estimated by "head-
counting" the share of low-income beneficiaries.

The methodology did not allow measurement of the distributional impact of all projects. In fact, about a third of all loans were normal-
ly not assessed. This severed the methodology from the mandate since
the low-income goal was intended to apply to the whole of the lending program. Moreover, the methodology measures expected distribution of benefits. (Few ex post facto analyses are available from which
to draw firm conclusions.) Finally, the cost-benefit methodology and
head-counting showed different results. The difference could be attributed either to the method itself or to the distributional impact. Because
head-counting was used mainly in social development projects, it is

probable that the better performance of these projects was due more to their distributional impact than to measurement problems, but the latter could not be discounted.

Nonetheless, the findings contained in the Bank's own assessment of its experience followed expected trends and produced predictable results. First, it was easier for the Bank to meet the target before the debt crisis. The 50 percent target was met without difficulties before 1982 without an active promotion of particular projects. It was not met after 1982, when financial survival and fiscal stringency overrode social expenditures that had a direct impact on low-income groups. It has not been met since 1986 even when emphasis in social sectors was rekindled. During 1987–1989 the portfolio had a distributional effect of 44 percent (up from 35 percent in the 1983–1985 period). This means that, despite the priority given to low-income levels, the target is not easily fulfilled. Countries may have other overriding considerations or may choose to undertake social investments with other resources. In these circumstances the Bank was not able to fulfill its mandate.

Second, there are predictable sector differences. Projects for agriculture, urban development, and health showed higher proportions of benefits to low-income groups than energy generation, industry, or transportation projects[2] (see Table 5.1).

Table 5.1    Estimate of Distribution of Benefits to Low-Income Private Agents from Bank Pipeline: 1990–1993

| Sector | Distributional Impact 1983–1989 (%) | Pipeline 1990–1993[a] Number | Pipeline 1990–1993[a] $ Millions | Low-Income Estimated Benefits to Groups ($ Millions) |
|---|---|---|---|---|
| Agriculture | 55 | 43 | 2,155 | 1,185 |
| Fisheries | 59 | 1 | 100 | 59 |
| Forestry | 20 | 6 | 236 | 46 |
| Industry | 26 | — | — | — |
| Tourism | 82 | 4 | 420 | 346 |
| Mining | 48 | 2 | 190 | 91 |
| Energy | 18 | 21 | 2,771 | 504 |
| Transportation | 25 | 30 | 2,505 | 617 |
| Communication | 83 | — | — | — |
| Urban development | 75 | 18 | 1,299 | 979 |
| Science and technology | 91 | — | — | — |
| Education | 73 | 17 | 551 | 402 |
| Health | 82 | 24 | 1,152 | 941 |
| Environment | 50 | 16 | 740 | 370 |
| Other | 90 | — | — | — |
| Total | — | 214 | 14,202 | 6,568 |

Source: IDB database. Pipeline as of October 1990.
Note: a. Includes only those projects where IDB's distributional analysis methodology is applicable.

Finally, there is a tendency for projects in the poorest countries (Group D) to show higher proportions of low-income beneficiaries. This may be partly due to a higher proportion of poor people in the population; it also indicates a higher share of Bank lending for social projects in these countries. The availability of concessional funds for these countries has typically made social loans more attractive to them than to countries that opted for using fiscal resources. Group A countries, for example, did not borrow from the IDB for health projects until after the debt crisis erupted. Mexico and Argentina joined the list only in 1986.

In sum, the low-income mandate had many loopholes. Loan officers were sensitive to the overall target and were aware that compliance required that the borrowing program in every country take that target into consideration, but individual operations were not preselected for their distributional impact. The goal remained a vaguely couched wish without the support of broader poverty-oriented policies and unaccompanied by instruments for implementation. There was no requirement to give special weight to low-income benefits in resource programming and in project design. In essence, the Bank was expected to move toward the target without changing its way of doing business.

Nevertheless, the proposal for the Sixth Replenishment in 1983 retained the commitment and further stated that "the Bank will continue to make every effort to assure that the impact of lending operations accrues to the benefit of low income groups, whenever possible" (IDB, *Proposal for the Sixth General Increase*, 1978, 29). It was agreed that the ex ante evaluation of the distributive impact should be continued and that, as projects under the previous replenishment reached completion stage, ex post facto evaluations should gauge the validity of the methodology. The Seventh Replenishment completed in 1989 further emphasized that "the Bank will do its utmost to ensure that 50 percent of its lending program should be allocated to benefit the lower income groups" (IDB, *Proposal for the Seventh General Increase*, 1989, 13).

A preferential financial matrix was created to support this goal. The shares of total costs that could be funded by the IDB would be supplemented by an additional ten percentage points for projects that provided at least 50 percent of their benefits to low-income groups. For the first time, there was incentive for borrowers to design or redesign projects with a high proportion of low-income beneficiaries. This was a modest attempt to address the disjuncture between the processes of project selection and project design to meet the low-income target. The Bank nonetheless faced "significant obstacles in reaching this objective" (IDB, *Review of the Low Income Goal*, rev. 1990, 8) for several reasons. In part, this is due to the lack of a coherent strategy to pursue the mandate. In part, the mandate itself is contradictory. Shareholders push divergent views for replenishment guidelines; the resulting mandate is the product of negotiation, not a coherent development philosophy. Moreover, as development objectives increase in complexity, more demands are made over time. The Bank's agenda has become increasingly overloaded, pulling the Bank in different—sometimes even opposing—directions. Overloading may satisfy all actors at the bargaining table, but it does not contribute to a more effective loan program.

Thus, while the low-income goal was retained for the total lending program, other directions were superimposed for the use of resources as a result of the Seventh Replenishment. First, adjustment loans were allocated a share of 25 percent despite the difficulty of ascertaining their distributional impact. Second, the requirement to cofinance with the World Bank meant that the IDB lost some control over project selection and design. Third, 65 percent of the resources were allocated to Group A and B countries, which do not have access to the subsidized IFF or to the concessional FSO.[3] The core of the lending program with these countries is adjustment operations and infrastructure or directly productive activities. Last, the Bank's evolving mandate also singled out special emphasis for the environment, export promotion, science, and technology, in which benefits to low-income groups are likely to be small or lacking.

Historically, fulfillment of the goal was assessed vis-à-vis measurable lending, which was equivalent to two-thirds of total lending. But the proportion of measurable loans declined for the Seventh Replenishment. Half or more of the Bank's lending over the 1990–1993 period was destined for programs and projects not assessed for distributional impact, either because the methodology did not allow it or it was not cost efficient (for example, adjustment loans, energy generation projects, global credits, and preinvestment loans). Under routine criteria, that is, if only the measurable lending was considered, the goal was not reached. In sum, only one-half of the loans could be assessed, and of these an average 40 percent of the benefits reached low-income groups (IDB, *Report on the Eighth General Increase*, 1994).

The Bank recommended to the Programming Committee in 1990 (CP-141) that they consider the directions spelled out in the 1990 *World Development Report* (World Bank 1990): improved access to education, nutrition, health care, and other social services, so that benefits to the poor were included in project selection and design. The report concluded that the best way to increase benefits to low-income groups would be to emphasize a multidimensional framework using poverty reduction and social policy issues in the programming process and country dialogue; enhancing poverty reduction through project design, including improved targeting of benefits; and reforming social sectors for greater scope and delivery of social services and institutional support.

Steered by the president, an improved social strategy is now on the table. A dialogue on social reform, akin to the country dialogue that took place on adjustment, would entail more than Bank lending. The Bank must become a forum for regional consensus and use its clout to define actions for poverty reduction that include an increased mobilization of internal resources.

Beyond this activist strategy, adaptation of current policies is also being undertaken. First, ex ante measurements of poverty impact were modified for the Eighth Replenishment. There will be greater emphasis on distributional impact as a criteria, first for project selection and then for project design. A review and update of the break-off points for the definition of low-income segments in each country has been undertaken. Third, employment creation for people on the border of poverty is crucial, and a key element is expansion of the microenterprise program to enable the poor to capitalize.

The Eighth Replenishment, which was completed in 1994, carried the mandate that 40 percent of the volume of loans and 50 percent[4] of the total number of Bank operations be dedicated to social reform and poverty reduction. It introduced the possibility of financing a share of the recurrent costs of social projects on a case-by-case basis. This would allow the Bank to directly mitigate the adverse effects of adjustment on the most vulnerable groups.[5]

In addition to more lending, the Bank should be encouraged to shift its emphasis from traditional social sector projects to the reshaping of social and taxation policies. The measures will not have an immediate impact, but taken together they should enable the Bank (and the region) to move forward in effective ways.

The region has more poor people today than at the beginning of the 1980s, both in absolute numbers and as a share of the total population. The number of poor increased by 50 million over the estimated 130 million in 1980. Over the decade the region's long-standing problem with income distribution has worsened. The best solution lies in policy reform (Cardoso and Helwege 1992).

Social reform is a bottom-up process. The Bank cannot be a substitute for domestic efforts, but it can and must be a catalyst. A social and political consensus on the need to provide and direct public resources to fight poverty is a precondition for the transfer of resources from one powerful group of the population to another less powerful. In other words, society must be led to feel a strong aversion to poverty, a task for which the Bank is well placed.

## New Institutional Organization[6] _____

The Bank's present organization is the result both of interplay between BMCs and non-BMCs and of the renewal of the Bank's agenda at the Seventh Replenishment. During 1988 a thorough assessment of the Bank's structure and operations was carried out by a high-level review committee and three task forces (which reviewed human resources and overall administration of the Bank, general and sectoral policy objectives, and operational modalities). On the basis of their conclusions, management produced its own proposals for reforms in the areas of policies, operational procedures, and human resource administration (IDB, *Basic Management Proposals*, 1989).

The Bank reorganization changed both structure and processes to manage the increased transfer of resources and to support resource mobilization in the BMCs. In the medium term, the Bank assisted the BMCs in their efforts to modernize and to restore growth. It expanded the scope and increased the frequency of its dialogue with the BMCs to enhance its catalytic role in resource mobilization. The reorganization was completed in 1990.

The major achievement of the reorganization was to strengthen the process of country programming and the Bank's capacity for policy-based lending. In the department of plans and programs (DPL), a sector lending and policy division now guides adjustment lending. The organization changed from one devoted exclusively to financing investment projects to one whose dialogue with BMCs included the economic and financial policy framework that shaped projects. Country programming and country dialogue are now carried out with an interdepartmental team approach.

### The Project Cycle

Project ideas may originate in the BMC or in the Bank, either at headquarters or from the field office. In principle, programming at the Bank starts with the socioeconomic report produced independently by the economic and social development department. This provides the basis for the country programming paper (CPP) (prepared by an interdepartmental working team chaired by DPL), which lays out the lending strategy. This paper becomes the basis for identifying financing priorities that consider the objectives and financing programs of other bilateral and multilateral development institutions.[7] The CPP does not need Board approval. Based on the CPP, country teams identify projects that embody the policies, strategies, and priorities resulting from the programming phase.

The appropriate operations department division chief heads the country team, which also includes a country office representative, a programming officer of DPL, a country economist of the social and economic development department (DES), and a representative of the project analysis department (PRA).

The country team presents a profile of potential projects to the programming committee chaired by the president. The profile is reviewed and agreed upon with country authorities. High-level Bank officials, sometimes headed by the president or the vice president, visit the country and meet with the Finance Ministry, the Ministry of the Economy, or the Ministry of Planning to obtain strategic agreements. The type and volume of future loans are negotiated. The Bank can take the initiative and make suggestions on the priorities identified. Ultimately the country will make a decision and request specific loans, but the Bank can pursue its own mandate, although the degrees of freedom may vary from country to country. In any case the mandate is a composite, and its ultimate application is meant to be flexible. Bank staff report back to the programming committee, whose task it is to match country lending with Bank priorities.

In all operations, a profile of the project idea is prepared by the country team and submitted to the programming committee for approval. Upon approval the project becomes a part of the "pipeline." In investment loans, the country team prepares a second profile that further defines the operation and enables management's loan committee to determine whether to dedicate resources for project preparation and analysis. The loan committee is chaired by the executive vice president, by convention a U.S. national.

Once the loan committee has determined that an operation warrants further development, an interdepartmental team of specialists, the project team, is formed. The composition and leadership of the project team depends on the type of operation: investment project, policy based, a hybrid of the two, small project, or technical cooperation. The project team analyzes and negotiates the operation with country authorities. When agreement is reached, the loan proposal goes back to the loan committee and then to the Board. The whole process takes from eighteen to twenty-four months.

The establishment of country and project teams has contributed to better coordination between departments. Prior to the reorganization, the CPP did not influence decisionmaking much; the Bank's strategy in a particular country has now been streamlined. This tighter process of country programming has increased the transparency of the pipeline and set priorities on operations. One criticism has been that "solidarity between borrowers has been eroded."[8] However, the team approach has given a more comprehensive view of the project.

Decisionmaking has devolved to middle management. According to interviews with the professional staff, this is one of the major achievements of the Bank's reorganization. Still, the need to reach a consensus is cumbersome and slows down the process, while the need to accommodate all viewpoints contributes to a complex design.

As part of the discussions for the Eighth Replenishment, the president set up a task force on portfolio management problems of the IDB. The six-member task force, headed by Moeen A. Qureshi, became known informally as TAPOMA (taskforce on portfolio management). The report found that portfolio management was hampered by the bureaucratic nature of the project cycle. The system led to excessive layers of supervision and redundant vertical and lateral clearances "as project teams strive to produce error-free products capable of responding to all possible concerns which might be raised by senior management and the Board" (IDB, *Managing for Effective Development*, 1993, 16). Moreover, no single department held responsibility for a loan; accountability was reduced. It discouraged personal initiative and responsibility. Some borrowers, moreover, report that the team approach complicated the dialogue because there was no single interlocutor for a loan. The Bank is further reorganizing to act on these findings. It is expected that the country focus of operations will be strengthened so that yearly "country papers" can be presented to the Board reviewing the country portfolio and planned areas of cooperation (IDB, *Report on the Eighth General Increase*, 1994).

### New Priorities, New Divisions

Five new divisions were created to take up the special lending activities established at the Seventh Replenishment: environment, microenterprises, human capital development, integration and regional cooperation, and cofinancing and export promotion lending. The last three were slow to get started; strategies were more active for microenterprises and the environment. The microenterprise division in the department of operations and the environment division in the project analysis department outperformed the others. The microenterprise division is small, especially in terms of the region's need to create employment, offset fragmented domestic capital markets, and create opportunities for the poor to obtain credit. All in all, the Seventh Replenishment approved four hundred operations for a total of $322 million. Besides the granting of credit, the legal and regulatory context of microenterprises was studied in several countries for future loan planning.

The environmental protection division is highly regarded both within and outside the Bank. It is staffed by twenty professionals subdivided into two groups; one dealing with the quality control of operations and the other with promoting and developing environmental operations. In addition, the division has developed operation guidelines and procedures, conducted training seminars both at HQ and country offices, and integrated environmental responsibilities among various departments and offices. Technical assistance has also been provided to improve local capabilities in the management of the environment.

In the course of the Seventh Replenishment, $3.6 billion, or 15 percent of lending, was approved for environmental protection. In 1992 and 1993 there was a major increase to ten projects totaling $2.2 billion. Among these was the project to decontaminate the Tiete River in São Paulo, Brazil, which is the largest loan approved by the Bank.[9] The project to clean up the river was in response to massive public demand and an organized public campaign by local NGOs (Schwartzman 1994). In Brazil, the Bank also supports the National Environmental Fund, the first loan in which the Bank and a government agreed on a financial mechanism for grassroots NGOs and small municipalities.

Besides massive clean-up of the local environment, the Bank is strengthening local institutions and NGOs. The IDB is also using seminars to present the legal and institutional changes required by the 1992 Rio Conference.

An environment committee examines all projects in the first phases of the project cycle. Operations are classified into four categories depending upon the environmental impact predicted. Environmental policies have been applied successfully by the project teams, although environmental issues are still not consistently incorporated into the programming process.

Environmental specialists are not restricted to the environment division. There are twenty professionals in other units who use their experience in environmental issues to coordinate with the division. Six regional specialists have been recruited for the field offices. Several environmentalists have been recruited from NGOs in an effort to incorporate their concerns. Currently, the IDB devotes more financial and personnel resources to environmental concerns than any other regional development bank. The Bank's fast buildup of skills in the field and its partnership with NGOs have been commended.

## Loan Quality

The IDB had two separate units to cover different aspects of ex post facto evaluation until 1993. The Office of Review and Evaluation (ORE) was established under Board jurisdiction in 1968. The

Operations Evaluation Office (OEO), within the administrative structure of the Bank, was opened in 1974. It was in charge of all ex post facto evaluations of operations. In contrast, ORE reviewed policies, procedures, and organizations including operations and the work of OEO. ORE specialized in identifying problems in the project cycle. OEO provided feedback on projects, but it came late in the process of loan preparation, after issues had already been resolved or could not be resolved. The operational units, moreover, were inconsistent in accepting findings or recommendations. This attitude led many operational officers to adopt a negative view of the evaluation function (IDB, *Revised Report*, 1989, 42).

Moreover, the existence of the two units gave rise to competition and left important gaps. Only ex post facto evaluations were done. Experience gained by one sector was not gathered and disseminated to others. Studies were not designed to provide an estimate of portfolio performance. They covered projects with problems of performance and were designed to guide future operations.

Complaints over the quality of IDB loans in the 1980s were widespread, particularly from the U.S. Treasury. There was consensus that the physical aspects of projects were satisfactory and that failures were related to factors outside the project, but knowledge was fragmentary. Especially vulnerable to criticism were the large energy projects characteristic of all multilateral development banks after the oil shocks of the 1970s. The IDB experienced both success and failure on this score (see country studies on Costa Rica and Argentina in Chapter 4).

Policy-based lending was introduced to address the macroeconomic conditions and reduce the distortions that affect projects. The arrival of new management in 1989 and the overall restructuring of the Bank reduced complaints from the United States about the quality of projects that abounded in the late 1980s. But other problems that dealt with internal Bank policies and procedures remained.

A 1992 staff survey remarked that changes in project analysis to enhance quality control remained inadequate after the reorganization. The project advisory office, which was to develop and update methodologies and supervise their application, did not live up to its promise. The office had only produced a "synopsis of existing practice" for certain sectors such as energy, water and sewerage, and urban projects. The staff surveyed also pointed out that the office was mainly composed of economists and thus "too geared to economic analysis in terms of quality" (IDB, *Assessment of the IDB*, 1992, 25), omitting consideration of financial, technical, and institutional aspects.

The lack of an independent evaluation unit was viewed as one of the most obvious weaknesses of the Bank. Many shareholders had reservations about the objectivity and credibility of operations. To resolve the problems, the president established the portfolio management task force known as TAPOMA in 1993 as mentioned earlier. The TAPOMA report was a milestone. Because the available information and the historical evaluation output were lacking, TAPOMA's terms of reference were different from a similar exercise carried out at the World Bank, the report under the direction of W. Wapenhans (World Bank, *Effective Implementation,* 1993). TAPOMA was not able to document a decline in the quality of the IDB's loan portfolio, as did the Wapenhans report for the World Bank. Nonetheless, TAPOMA produced an insightful and incisive review of portfolio management at the IDB. Its findings and conclusions, more qualitative than quantitative, are useful and have provoked an immediate reaction.

The task force assessed a sample of projects approved under the Seventh Replenishment for the adequacy of economic, technical, and institutional analyses. It concluded that "projects appear to be sound and are broadly meeting their intended objectives . . . economic analyses in particular were of high quality and technical analyses appeared sound. Institutional analyses, especially those related to assessing the capacity of proposed implementing agencies, were weak" (IDB, *Managing for Effective Development,* 1993, 10).

The task force stressed that the available information did not allow a complete assessment of the portfolio's contribution to development. The Bank's approach to project execution emphasized control—control over disbursements, compliance with procurement rules and contracting, compliance with conditionality, and adherence to procedures. Financial accountability was the preeminent concern in the assessment of results.

The source of the problem was that the internal evaluation system was primarily geared to draw lessons to improve project preparation and analysis in the BMCs and quality at the point of entry. OEO provided direct feedback to all new projects, but it failed to track problems during execution. The Bank's information on the status of active projects was narrowly focused on monitoring the performance of BMCs and the progress toward achievement of execution benchmarks (procurement, availability of counterpart funds, timely signature of contracts, and so on). Information on past operations stemmed from four basic documents: the project completion reports (PCRs) and borrowers ex post evaluations (BEPs) and operation evaluation reports and project performance reports. These were not comprehensive documents with reliable findings, conclusions, and recommendations. PCRs varied widely in terms of quality and content; because they were unaudited no clear lessons could be extracted. Submission of BEPs, a contractual condition, was not always achieved because of institutional weaknesses in borrowing member countries.

At the end of 1992 the double evaluation system was eliminated, and a new unit was created. This new evaluation office answers to the Board and the president on the development effectiveness of the Bank, on the portfolio quality, and the transparency and accountability of projects and programs. It is responsible for reviews and evaluations of policies, programs, systems, procedures, and projects, including evaluation of projects in execution, examination of PCRs and BEPs, and impact evaluations, both immediately upon final disbursement and a number of years after project completion. It will disseminate the results of evaluations to country offices and headquarters to ensure that they are used in the project cycle.

Evaluations must function as a corporate tool for institutional learning; recommendations from its findings must be disseminated and incorporated into projects in a timely fashion. The move is desirable per se; moreover, it could be the basis for relieving the Board of the need to revise minutely the terms for the approval of loans.

### From Quantity to Quality: How Feasible?

The attainment of development goals has hinged on following timely issues and on satisfying shareholders' priorities. Divisions were created to tackle new issues, such as microenterprises and export promotion. As layers were added, the integration of policy priorities in all Bank activities suffered. This is a key factor affecting quality and impact on development that must be tracked in the future. A consistent country assistance strategy should contribute to this task. As the portfolio shifts away from bulky, capital-intensive projects toward support of weaker social sectors, follow-up and durability of results will be increasingly important.

Concern with quality over quantity may be facilitated as the Bank moves from a four-year funding cycle to a sustainable level of lending that allows the Bank to function without periodic replenishments. As the Bank achieves a sustainable level of funding, a coherent lending philosophy may blossom. Scrutiny may be left to the independent evaluation unit. Quality thrives in a healthy atmosphere; it cannot survive perpetual renegotiation and the pressure to fill targets. Given room for intellectual growth and for tapping the analytical resources in the region, the Bank can take on a more enterprising role.

The goals of social equity and poverty reduction require specific and numerous "home grown" policy interventions. A more flexible approach to the transfer of resources will be required. Bank lending needs to be tailored to long-term programs; extended grace, disbursement, and amortization periods need to be considered. The new businesses can lead to lower loan volumes and to more staff-intensive operations than the Bank and its BMCs have been used to. Not only can lower profit margins be expected, but the trend will be to negative transfers with the BMCs after a few years.[10] The leverage of the Bank will be reduced, should capital inflows not be reversed. One can only speculate about the future state of flows to regional BMCs, but it is possible that technical cooperation instead of massive resource transfer will need to become a central part of the Bank's business, particularly to support social policy reform, institution building, and strengthening human resource development, environmental protection, regional trade, and integration. Further down the road, devolution of responsibilities to more-developed borrowing member countries must be considered.

## Notes

1. For the limits of this methodology, see IDB, *Evaluation Review on IDB's Experience under the Low Income Goal*, RE-139 (1986).

2. This draws from IDB, RE-139 (1986) and CP-141 (1990).

3. They do have access, however, to FSO resources in their local currencies, which are part of their own contributions.

4. This represents a considerable increase from the Seventh Replenishment levels. Social sectors represented 25 percent of total lending in the 1991–1994 period, up from 15 percent during the 1970s.

5. The World Bank finances certain incremental recurrent costs, mainly training, on a declining basis, but this change poses several dilemmas. The move will require management to consider changes in loan processing and the incorporation of new skills. Not all BMCs will be inclined to increase their external debt obligations to finance recurrent costs.

6. The Bank also undertook a major reorganization at the time of writing.

7. Resource transfer was identified as the major problem to be addressed by the Seventh Replenishment. Since then the paper has emphasized macro variables. It is expected that in the future there will be more emphasis on the needs of the poor to accompany the new Bank strategy for social reform and poverty.

8. Confidential interview.

9. A decade earlier the largest loan was delivered to Yacyreta, the Argentine-Paraguayan hydroelectric dam on the Parana River. See the Argentina country study in Chapter 4.

10. The IDB is the only official lender expected to hold positive net flows with the region in the immediate future.

# 6

# COMPARATIVE ADVANTAGE
# AND REGIONAL LEADERSHIP

This chapter analyzes the de facto and de jure division of labor between the IDB and the World Bank after the Seventh Replenishment in 1989. In subsequent sections it assesses how this has worked in policy-based lending and in lending to social sectors. The last section describes the ways in which the IDB strives to provide regional leadership.

The dilemmas inherent in institutional diversification and overlapping responsibilities are not new. "When the lending countries accepted the establishment of regional development banks, they were fully aware that the purposes of these new agencies would, to some extent, overlap with those of the World Bank. These countries were prepared, however, to see a certain pluralism in multilateral aid policies and practices introduced in the interest of creating institutions that would specialize in the problems of particular areas and in order to give the developing countries a greater sense of participation and identification" (Dell 1972, 30).

The Bank's first president stated that the Bank should function as "a university of development." The IDB set a tradition of providing an intellectual alternative to the Bretton Woods institutions. As established by its Articles, its mandate was to finance "principally projects, including those forming part of a national or regional development program" (Article III, section 7.a.iv). The IDB was required to provide technical assistance "for the preparation, financing and implementation of development plans, including the study of priorities" (Article I, section 2.a.v). The Bank worked in a policy milieu that attached a high value to state planning. At the behest of the Alliance for Progress, countries engaged in national planning exercises. These were then examined by "nine wise men" at the Inter-American Committee for the Alliance for Progress in the OAS. National econom-

95

ic authorities complied with these exercises with varying degrees of enthusiasm, depending on the political complexion of their governments.[1]

At first the IDB and the World Bank competed with each other. To avoid conflict and disagreements, informal sectoral agreements were worked out to guide operations. In education, for example, there was an agreement that included not only both banks but also USAID. The IDB undertook loans for higher education, the World Bank concentrated on the secondary level, and USAID supported the primary level. Coordination was mostly restricted to avoiding duplication rather than joint forward planning or collaboration on program formulation or execution. The IDB subsequently expanded its policy to an all-level approach to education, and the World Bank moved into primary and nonformal technical education. But there is no evidence of integrated planning concerning the shift in each bank's activities (IDB, *Review and Evaluation System*, 1978). At the country level, the division of labor between the banks was part of each country's public sector investment programs.

Since the 1970s there has been an increasing convergence of views and policies. The IDB's lending for social projects declined as a share of total lending while the World Bank, under the basic human needs thrust, moved into areas pioneered by the IDB. With the passage of time, the differences between the institutions narrowed, each one adapting ideas and practices from the other. Stabilization and adjustment became a preoccupation. Williamson (1990) characterized the reform scheme as the "Washington consensus." The IDB, under the direction of President Iglesias, warned against "counterproductive dichotomies" and promoted a pragmatic convergence of ideas (Iglesias 1992).

## Relations with the World Bank

The mandate of the Seventh Replenishment drew the IDB closer to the World Bank. Prior to it there were about three or four joint operations per year. These jumped to sixteen out of a total of fifty-two in 1991 and included both investment and adjustment operations. In 1992 the number fell to seven. In the large countries where it has less leverage, the IDB accepts, implicitly, the focus of IMF–World Bank programs on exchange rate, trade policy, and other price issues. It avoids giving conflicting advice or stipulating conflicting conditions. This is outlined in the country programming paper from which the project pipeline is subsequently designed. At the same time the Bank can emphasize issues of public investment and public expenditure in sector adjustment operations.

In the small countries where the IDB is more knowledgeable than the other IFIs and is an important (and many times, the main) provider of external funds, programmatic differences are more frequent. The IDB broke new ground in Jamaica when it stipulated devaluation as a precondition for its 1991 investment sector loan, despite there being an IMF program in place that did not include an exchange rate adjustment. In that case, the IDB was able to convince the IMF to follow its advice.[2] However, in Barbados the exchange rate adjustment proposed by the IDB was opposed by the IMF for reasons of timing. The IDB decided to accept the IMF argument; devaluation was not made a condition of the IDB investment sector loan.

High-level coordination between the IDB and the World Bank has been strengthened after the Seventh Replenishment, facilitated by headquarters of both banks in Washington. The need to tighten coordination has been tackled without a formal memorandum of understanding between both banks, perhaps because, on the whole, relations in Washington at the senior management level tend to be good, and there is a wish for close cooperation in both banks. The World Bank's vice president for Latin America and the IDB's president, accompanied by managers of operational departments, have periodic meetings to discuss country perspectives and operations. There are also periodic meetings between both banks' country division chiefs, together with IDB managers or deputy department managers, to discuss the schedule and goals of joint operations. It had originally been proposed to draft a formal memorandum of understanding for sharing responsibilities. The proposal was dismissed as impractical. Some shareholders resist the potential loss of procurement if they are members of the World Bank but not of the IDB; BMCs also favor a degree of competition between lending agencies. An aide-memoire to direct joint operations now guides officials, and it seems to be satisfactory for both sides.

Clearly the effectiveness of this mechanism hinges on the individuals involved. Moreover, if cofinancing declines, the need to formalize relations may increase to avoid contradictory directions. To the present, cofinancing allowed the IDB to rely on the World Bank and IMF for the existence of an appropriate macro framework. In the future, as it finances adjustment operations progressively on its own, the IDB will need a clearer picture of the macro framework as determined by the World Bank and the IMF, both as a prerequisite for lending and for implementation. The inclusion of the IDB in the framing of the policy framework papers (PFPs)[3] can enhance the effectiveness of adjustment lending and can avoid the risk of conflicting advice.

In sum, relations with the World Bank can be characterized as cooperative in the case of the large countries and competitive in the case of the small ones. Generally, greater absorptive capacity and an abundance of good projects minimizes jealousy and political conflict, and cooperation is facilitated as each institution brings to the relationship a strength that the other lacks. Where this is not possible, differences have been resolved by a sectoral division of labor. Policy-based lending, however, requires that solutions be found in designing programs.

In the small countries, programmatic differences are frequent because the IDB has historically had a prolonged presence and more important lending programs. The World Bank is the newcomer here with a smaller lending program. Difficulties arise when circumstances require the World Bank to abdicate the role of lead institution. Guyana is a case in point. Field relations among project officers in these circumstances were exceedingly competitive, with accusations of highjacking, project piracy, or skimming off the best parts of projects. Conflict arose when, after years of building and working with a team, the IDB found its executing agency taken over by the World Bank's incoming program.

On the whole, synergy exists between the regional bank and the Bretton Woods institutions; major divergences in policy tend to be discouraged. In many cases the BMCs also actively encourage coordination.

Notwithstanding the convergence of the policies of the multilateral banks in recent years, the IDB has carved a role for itself that is distinct from, yet not in dissonance with, the World Bank. The IDB retains a certain individuality as a result of its background, its character as a regional institution, and its more microscopic focus. There are several ways in which this is reflected.

### Tighter Net: Small Countries, Small Projects

The IDB has specialized in lending to the small countries. Not only did it target and reach the small countries left out of the World Bank's wider net; it also lent more on a per capita basis to the small and poor countries (Griffith-Jones et al. 1994).[4] The country distribution of IDB and World Bank lending after the debt crisis also shows that the latter lent more, both in absolute terms and as a share of its total loans, to the large countries in the region (Groups A and B). The IDB, on the other hand, specialized in lending to the small C and D countries in the region. (See Table 6.1 and Figure 6.1.)

Based on the small-country focus of the RDBs and the danger of overlapping and duplication among the multilateral banks, there have been proposals for the World Bank to concentrate on the big countries where it has more clout, while the RDBs concentrate exclusively on small countries where they have more knowledge and leverage. The

Table 6.1    IDB and World Bank Lending Operations in Latin America Compared by Country Groups: 1984–1992 (amounts in U.S.$ millions)

| Year | A and B | | C and D | | Total | |
|------|---------|-----|---------|-----|-------|-----|
| | IDB[a] | WB[b] | IDB[a] | WB[b] | IDB[a] | WB[b] |
| 1984 | 2,248.8 | 2,765.3 | 1,070.8 | 263.6 | 3,319.6 | 3,028.9 |
| 1985 | 1,914.1 | 3,316.5 | 1,071.3 | 381.7 | 2,985.4 | 3,698.2 |
| 1986 | 1,647.3 | 4,238.3 | 1,321.3 | 532.9 | 2,968.6 | 4,771.2 |
| 1987 | 1,315.4 | 4,429.3 | 971.2 | 722.7 | 2,286.6 | 5,152.0 |
| 1988 | 1,076.7 | 4,731.0 | 524.5 | 533.0 | 1,601.2 | 5,264.0 |
| 1989 | 1,653.8 | 5,118.5 | 899.1 | 723.6 | 2,552.9 | 5,842.1 |
| 1990 | 2,832.0 | 5,206.7 | 971.3 | 658.0 | 3,803.3 | 5,864.7 |
| 1991 | 3,533.5 | 4,446.5 | 1,796.8 | 787.2 | 5,330.3 | 5,233.7 |
| 1992 | 4,214.8 | 4,804.2 | 1,776.8 | 857.3 | 5,991.6 | 5,661.5 |

Source: IDB, President's Report to the Board, 1992.
Notes: a. Calendar years.
b. Fiscal years.

arguments in favor of this division of labor are not persuasive in the case of the IDB, despite its small-country focus. Some doubts have been expressed by IDB staff on the extent to which this relative emphasis on small countries can be maintained because of the high overhead costs of the Bank. It takes the Bank up to $1 million to prepare a loan; small loans below $50 million are not cost effective.[5]

To continue to lend to small countries and become more efficient, the IDB will have to on-lend more funds to, and work out tighter arrangements with, the subregional banks: the Caribbean Development Bank, the Andean Development Fund, and the Central American Bank for Economic Integration. Together they cover the medium and small BMCs in the region. The only countries not borrowing members of a subregional bank are three of the biggest countries in the region: Argentina, Brazil, and Mexico, as well as Chile, Uruguay, and Paraguay. This trend can be seen in Costa Rica where the Central American Bank for Economic Integration is expected to be a more important provider of funds than the World Bank in the immediate future.

The "small-lender" view of the IDB in relation to that of the World Bank is also reflected in some types of credit operations, such as its loans to microenterprises, which are delivered in two ways. First, in 1978 the Board approved the allocation of $5 million for a program to assist small enterprises with concessional funds. Individual projects were limited to $500,000. A year later the Board authorized continuation of the program indefinitely without the $5 million ceiling. Under this program the IDB does not collect its usual fee to cover administrative costs and does not require that repayment comply with

**Figure 6.1    IDB and World Bank Lending Operations in Latin America Compared by Country Groups: 1984–1992**

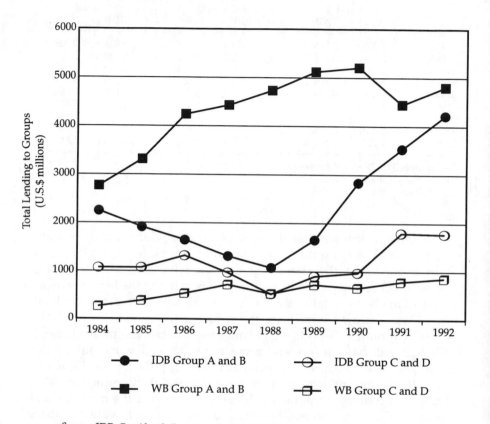

Source: IDB, *President's Report to the Board,* 1993.

maintenance of value obligations (in other words, payments or repayments in local currency when it has depreciated need not be compensated with additional local currency); however, credit terms to individual borrowers are at market rates. Unlike regular programs financed through the governments of BMCs, the small-projects program conveys its assistance mainly through private nonprofit organizations and in some instances through specialized public agencies (IDB, *IDB and Microenterprise,* 1991).

As its first showcase, the Bank selected Manos del Uruguay, a successful group of rural cooperatives in Uruguay composed of female artisans. In the course of ten years the program financed 103 projects in twenty-three countries for a total of $44.2 million. In addition, nearly $6 million in technical cooperation grants was awarded for training and institutional strengthening of intermediaries. The program was also successful in financial terms. Failure to pay off loans has been rare; arrears average 10 percent, and the default rate is well below 5 percent—a figure that compares favorably with the banking sector in general. This program also shows a small-country bias, with nearly three-quarters of funds going to Group C and D countries.

The small-projects program began as an experiment to finance unorthodox initiatives intended to reach the poor in productive activities. Financing was aimed at specific enterprises or regions within a BMC. Initially lending was done only for fixed assets. Subsequently, working capital and services were also covered. These measures allowed access by microentrepreneurs that included a high proportion of women. Even before the implementation of a strategy aimed at women in development (WID), the small-projects program is estimated to have reached 23,000 women representing 20 percent of all beneficiaries.

Mosley in Griffith-Jones et al. (1994) corroborated the conclusion that in the small-projects program in Bolivia women's organizations were well represented as beneficiaries. But he argued that the program should not be restricted to NGOs because these organizations traditionally lack accounting and general business skills.[6]

Based on the experience gained under the small-projects program, the Bank started a second program channeled through financial intermediaries in 1990. Global loans for microenterprises were introduced to allow disbursement of larger lending volumes. In the early small-projects program, the IDB allowed intermediaries to charge negative interest rates. Subsidization was found to generate excessive demand, and rationing was imposed through controls and cumbersome procedures. In contrast to previous operations, global loans are granted at market rates and are countrywide in scope. Although they involve larger sums of money to the country, much smaller loans are disbursed to the enterprises themselves. The loans are executed through a second-tier institution, such as a central or development bank, which channels the funds to the financial intermediaries. These lend directly to the microenterprises or to NGOs and cooperatives, which in turn lend the funds to their members or clients. The bulk of new lending to microentrepreneurs is now channeled through global loans. The first microenterprise bank in Latin America (in Bolivia) received an equity contribution from the IIC; more projects of this kind are under consideration.

### The NGO That Became a Bank

Banco Sol deserves to be regarded as the IDB's (formally the IIC's) most imaginative venture in lending to low-income groups. Founded in 1986 as PRODEM (Fondación para la Promocion y Desarrollo de la Microempresa, or Foundation for the Promotion and Development of Microenterprises), Banco Sol is the first NGO in the world to have successfully converted itself into a commercial bank. It makes initial loans of around $100 to very poor microentrepreneurs, 75 percent of whom are female, and a preliminary analysis suggests that 28 percent of its clients may have been moved over the poverty line as a consequence of Banco Sol loans. PRODEM was sponsored initially by USAID, through a PL480 loan, another non-governmental organization including ACCION International and the Calmeadow Foundation of Canada, and the Bolivian Emergency Social Fund; one of its strengths has always been the depth of its support in the Bolivian business, and in particular banking, community. The design characteristics which appear to be largely responsible for its success are:

(i)   the practice of lending at a commercial, not a subsidized interest rate;
(ii)  an extremely intensive system of loan monitoring under which loan installments are paid each Monday and any overdue debtor automatically receives a visit from a loan officer the following Tuesday (this requires sophisticated information systems, in which Banco Sol has invested heavily);
(iii) the practice of lending to individuals only if they are members of "solidarity groups" of four to seven persons who will stand surety for them if they default on a loan. Members of such groups naturally add to the pressure for loan repayment which comes from bank staff, as none of them can receive a loan if any member of the group is in default;
(iv)  a heavy investment in staff training and motivation.

These factors, between them, enabled PRODEM to maintain a repayment rate above 99 percent throughout its six years of operation. However, considerations of long-term sustainability caused PRODEM's staff to wish to convert the institution into a proper bank, with facilities for taking savings from the general public. For this a large increase in PRODEM equity capital was required, and the Inter-American Investment Corporation was crucial in providing this, with an investment of $1,325,000 made in 1991. Banco Sol formally reopened for business as a commercial bank on January 24, 1992. It now has over 30,000 borrowers in four urban locations in Bolivia, and expects once again to be profitable (under its new constitution) in 1993. Its importance is not only as one of the few institutions which has made a success of lending to the urban poor, but also as a potential model for lending to the rural poor, a job hitherto done with conspicuous lack of success (Mosley in Griffith-Jones et al. 1994, 29).

In general, one drawback to these lines of credit is their small size in relation to those of the informal sector in almost all Latin American countries. Under the Seventh Replenishment, they amounted to a little under $300 million. These programs need to be expanded in recognition of their impact on poverty. In addition, the democratization of credit could lift the restraint imposed by the existence of imperfect capital markets. Both the small-projects program and the microenterprise program could make a contribution in this respect if they were significantly funded.

Looking ahead, the Bank is promoting a number of initiatives at a regional level. Technical cooperation at the regional level assists the Andean Group in establishing a customs union, improving the foreign trade information system of the Latin American Integration Association (LAIA), and strengthening the Latin American private trading organization. It is also encouraging the establishment of a technological development program linking science and industry modeled along the lines of Eureka in Europe. ENLACE (Entidad Latinoamericana Cientifico Empresaria—Latin American Scientific and Entrepreneurial Entity) bolsters cooperation among companies in different countries and between companies and research institutes in the field of advanced technology both inside and outside the region. ENLACE, in turn, has inspired a group of Latin American bankers to set up a financial network to support projects under the program.

By targeting small countries and developing operations that can be "tailor-made," the IDB can move away from large-scale infrastructure projects. Under the Seventh Replenishment, megaprojects fell to one-fifth of lending, down from more than two-thirds during the 1970s and 1980s (see Tables 3.4 and 3.5). This shift was caused by small-project lending and large policy-based loans. Both increased in relative and absolute terms, although large-scale adjustment lending is still far from dominating the Bank's portfolio. This trend is further analyzed in the next section.

So long as the need for financial transfers to its biggest borrowers was a dominant concern, the Bank was prevented from taking full advantage of its strengths in other areas. If adjustment becomes anchored in the largest BMCs, the room for further diversification must be expanded. In small-scale operations lies the uniqueness of the IDB, a feature that should be retained and enhanced. The Bank can give timely responses to changing needs and serve as a rapid deployment force. Being in the region means that communication between lender and borrower is enhanced, and conditionalities can be designed and fine-tuned to different and changing needs.

## Development of Policy-Based Lending

Both in the literature on development finance and in loan statistics a distinction is made between project and program lending; yet that distinction is often blurred in practice. Project lending can be directed to a megaproject or to a series of interconnected projects. The IDB's involvement with sewerage and potable water is typical of this serial approach. In Argentina, for example, the participation of the IDB in this sector over a long period influenced public investment and policy formulation. Thus, such serial loans can be seen as precursors of modern sectoral loans—despite the obvious differences in conditionalities and disbursement procedures.

It can be argued that the first incursions of the IDB into aspects of policy-based lending started early, as a result of the Alliance for Progress. The Bank was entrusted with tax and agrarian reform support, but the extent to which it could induce policy changes was very limited. The Bank faced internal political obstacles in most countries so that few tax reforms were implemented. Substantially more funds were devoted to the colonization of new rural areas than to restructuring land tenure systems. An exception was a $20 million loan to Chile in the mid-1960s in support of President Eduardo Frei's program to provide 30,000 beneficiaries with credit facilities. The beneficiaries were small farmers who had been allocated between six and twenty hectares each and whose income was below $300 a year. The loans were channeled through new communal institutions operated by the beneficiaries themselves. The Bank also financed studies, technical assistance, and training of officials to plan and implement land reform programs.

Modern policy-based or adjustment-type loans were started almost ten years later at the IDB than at the World Bank and only after much soul-searching. There were concerns about the technical ability to undertake these operations, about the overlap with the Bretton Woods institutions, and about the risk that the image or identity of the Bank could be impaired by involvement in contentious issues.

Policy loans have been restricted to sector operations, in contrast to the World Bank, which has carried both sector adjustment loans and structural adjustment loans. The relative merits of each remains a matter of discussion; in the absence of a clear policy on the matter, the Bank's base of skills tilted the balance in favor of targeted interventions because knowledge on particular sectors was strong and could be put to use immediately. Macroeconomic capacity at the Bank needed to be expanded. As a result of the Seventh Replenishment, the Board of Governors authorized policy-based operations up to a ceiling of 25 percent of total loans over the period 1990–1993 (that is, U.S. $5.6 billion both from ordinary capital and the FSO).

The World Bank took on a temporary training role as the IDB moved into policy-based lending. The United States wanted the IDB to undertake parallel financing and work closely with the World Bank in policy-based loans for the first two years of the funding cycle to develop the necessary expertise. Potential areas of cooperation were extracted from the World Bank's pipeline at the country programming stage after Seventh Replenishment guidelines were approved and parallel financing procedures were put in place. Project teams were matched at the two banks. The IDB adopted the identical macro conditionality as that of the World Bank but used its own country analyses and objectives to spell out different conditions at the sector level. Supervision and periodic release of funds were closely coordinated and would not proceed over the objections of the World Bank (see World Bank, *Adjustment Lending by Regional*, 1992, 8).

The first sector loans were perforce restricted to operations in the World Bank's pipeline. The IDB's contributions to these first sector loans was limited. Moreover, the huge increase in the volume of lending that came with the Seventh Replenishment put pressure on management to get loans approved and "push the money out." This forced the staff to depend to a great extent on the World Bank. The requirement to undertake parallel financing with the World Bank led to a concentration of policy lending (and hence overall lending) in Group A and B countries, where the major thrust of World Bank policy lending in the region has gone. Gradually, as expertise was developed, the IDB focused on reforming sectors and state enterprises in which it had previous experience in project lending. The loan to Argentina to reform public enterprises concentrated on one sector, electric power, in which the IDB's strong expertise and background was put to use and which complemented the World Bank's efforts in other sectors.

The processing of adjustment operations was subjected to special review by the programming committee chaired by the president. The review concentrated on conditionality. Disbursement was generally split into two tranches. A third one could be added depending on the complexity of the project, timing concerns, and, above all, the financial needs of the BMC. In contrast with investment projects, which were monitored from the field offices, adjustment loans were supervised from the plans and programs department in Washington, D.C., a procedure initially meant to allow greater coordination with the World Bank. The release of all tranches required Board approval.

In late 1991, before the two-year learning period was completed, the United States agreed to drop the joint financing requirement. The Board gave its authorization to make sector loans independently of the World Bank on a case-by-case basis. Expertise has been developed through special training for existing staff and "aggressive recruitment" (IDB, *Mid-Term Report*, 1992). A network of consultants has also been established.[7] The move to independent lending was wise. The presence of the World Bank would be a drawback for adjustment operations planned in the coming years for the small Caribbean and Central American countries, where the experience of the IDB outpaces that of the World Bank. As can be inferred from Table 6.2, parallel financing with the World Bank fell during 1992. As expertise grew, the IDB's policy loans have not remained strictly sectoral. For example, it cofinanced the World Bank's SAL III in Costa Rica; in Bolivia its 1991 Multi-Sector Investment Loan is "a structural adjustment loan in all but name" (Mosley in Griffith-Jones et al. 1994). In Jamaica, the insistence on maintaining a high interest rate policy under an agricultural sector loan was bound to have an impact far beyond the sector, given the size and structure of the Jamaican economy.

**Table 6.2   Adjustment Lending (U.S.$ millions)**

|  | 1990 | 1991 | 1992 | 1993 |
| --- | --- | --- | --- | --- |
| Total lending | 3,832 | 5,359 | 6,023 | 5,962 |
| Adjustment lending | 1,310 | 2,050 | 1,500 | 494 |
| Share | 34% | 38% | 25% | 8% |
| Parallel with the World Bank | 1,310 | 1,700 | 180 | 80 |
| Share of adjustment lending parallel with the World Bank | 100% | 83% | 12% | 16% |

Source: IDB, *Annual Reports*.
Note: These figures do not correspond with those in Tables 3.4 and 3.5 because only "pure" fast-disbursing policy loans are included here.

The Bank was by now actively engaged in policy reform, and in three consecutive years it surpassed its loan approval record. It had been anticipated that sector lending would expand quickly, but in the first two years of implementation, it exceeded its 25 percent ceiling (although the ceiling was for the life of the replenishment). In 1990, the first year the lending modality was in operation, six sector loans to five countries were approved, totaling $1.3 billion, equaling 34 percent of the year's lending (see Table 6.2). The first sector loan was granted to Mexico for $300 million to finance policy reform in transportation and telecommunications. In telecommunications it assisted in the privatization of TELMEX and in establishing a new regulatory framework to promote and administer services. In transportation it assisted in the design of a new regulatory framework for freight hauling (IDB, *Annual Report*, 1991, 15). A public sector reform loan (also for $300 million) to Colombia was approved, while Venezuela received two loans for $300 million each—one to modernize the financial sector, the other for public enterprise reform. The financial sector loan includes policy actions such as improving credit allocation, reducing the role of the public sector in financial institutions, and establishing a stronger regulatory framework to supervise private banks. The public enterprise reform loan privatizes public firms and sets stricter operating rules for those in the public domain.

Agricultural sector loans were approved for Jamaica, Honduras, and Nicaragua. The loan to Honduras supported major reforms in the general policy environment, particularly relating to international trade. In Jamaica, the loan focused on pricing policies, agricultural credit (including interest rate policy), domestic marketing of important commodities such as cocoa and citrus, divestiture of publicly owned lands, and control of chemical pesticides.

In the cases of Venezuela and Mexico, the initiative for reform lay with the respective governments. The conditionalities posed few problems; indeed, the loans rewarded or consolidated past reforms. On the other hand, the policy reforms in Honduras and Jamaica raised contentious issues and led to delays. In the case of Jamaica, the Bank joined the World Bank, which was three years into its loan preparation, with excessive zeal; "its main contribution was related to the negotiation of interest rates" (IDB, *Two Years*, 1991, 34). While the World Bank had considered a reduction of subsidies to the agricultural sector, the IDB took a militant attitude and insisted on high positive real interest rates. The move was strongly opposed by the government, especially in relation to cocoa, banana, coffee, and citrus products. A "bitter dispute" ensued over the speed at which interest rates had to be raised for smallholdings (Levinson 1992). The Caribbean Development Bank also took issue with the IDB (Reid 1995). On efficiency grounds, the point of a positive interest rate policy was, to say the least, inconsistent with growth and recovery goals at a time when agriculture needed to be stimulated to generate output, employment, and foreign exchange. Moreover, no compensatory mechanisms were devised for low-income farmers. A more balanced approach was warranted instead of a conversion to the merits of efficiency for the sake of efficiency. This is precisely where the IDB should design appropriate, compassionate, intellectually creative conditionality, tailor-made to the political and social institutional idiosyncrasies of each BMC.

A link has been established between the IDB's adjustment loans and U.S. bilateral debt reduction. An investment sector loan (ISL) program, exclusive to the Bank and independent of the World Bank, has been started under the Enterprise for the Americas Initiative. As described by the Bank, the purpose of the program is to induce countries "to take steps to provide an investment environment conducive to private sector growth" (IDB, *Annual Report*, 1991, 23). The loan can serve as the basis for eligibility for the EAI: to qualify for debt relief under the EAI, "a country must first have in place the policy measures required by the ISL program, or otherwise be deemed by the Bank to be taking steps to create an investment climate favourable to private sector growth" (ibid). An investment sector loan is a large umbrella to cover "residual distortions" untouched by previous adjustment loans. Conditionalities are far-reaching and wide-ranging. Depending on the country and the circumstances, they can deregulate trade and finance, labor markets, securities markets, property rights (including intellectual property), and so on.

The design of the IDB's policy reform operations reinforces IMF/World Bank agreements and complements them in areas not under IMF/World Bank purview. For this reason, liaison with these programs, although not mandated, should be sought. In Costa Rica, the ISL program carries an informal agreement with the IMF as a precondition for disbursement. In Bolivia, the program builds on a financial sector loan of the World Bank; in turn, a public enterprise reform program from IDA was conceived as a second stage to the ISL program.

The first ISL was approved in June 1991 for Chile to receive U.S. $150 million. Loans for Jamaica, Bolivia, Colombia, Argentina, El Salvador, and Costa Rica were subsequently approved. The conditionality for Chile aims to open the copper and transportation sector to foreign investment, relax regulations on capital markets and investments by pension funds, sign inheritance tax and investment agreements, and pass legislation to allow international investment disputes to be resolved.

Many of these reforms were already being undertaken by the government of Chile. In fact, the loan proposal can hardly be described as a conditionality package because it was redundant, merely publicizing the reform process under way. Moreover, given the large financial inflows of recent years, the government was less interested in the funds per se than in being the first to sign a free trade agreement with the United States; and it was keen to obtain a "good housekeeping certificate" for the EAI. The unimportance of the funding was such that Chile asked for disbursements to be back-loaded so that the bulk would not be due at first tranche, as is customary. Subsequently, the government requested a one-year postponement of the release of the first tranche and an extension of the life of the loan to the end of 1994.

Chile's case may be exceptional. But there are other drawbacks if the creation of an adequate environment depends on legislation that is passed by a country's congress, not the executive branch that signs the loan contract. Chile may have a rare degree of consensus on reforms. In countries where the consensus is weaker and there is a properly functioning congress, the Bank may be caught in a dilemma. If the reform envisioned is not significant, the loan itself may be called into

### Ambitious Promises, Ambiguous Fulfillment

Conditionality is a sensitive instrument. For this reason legislative reform is included in the matrix in a rather ambiguous form. The conditionality matrix of the Argentine ISL exemplifies this problem. It anticipates vaguely couched commitments—"promises"—from the executive branch at the time of Board presentation. One example from the check list is intellectual property rights. Before Board presentation (and first tranche release), the executive branch is required to "present to Congress patent legislation that protects all products." No further policy measures are required (in this area) for second tranche release. At third tranche "adequate patent protection" must have been extended to all products, but there is no mention of enforcement or the sustainability of the policy. If such room for ambiguity must be left, perhaps it would be wiser for the Bank to include these reforms in the country dialogue and in the broad agreement on policy and institutional reform rather than tie them to disbursements.

The Argentine matrix holds other pitfalls. It is plagued with a proliferation of targets. Too many sectors, too many conditions, too many laws, and too many government agencies are intertwined. "The more policy targets and the more conditions any loan carries, the more problematic and weaker the enforcement of any individual condition tends to be" (Lewis 1993). In such circumstances the degree of compliance is not easy to ascertain at each disbursement. Synchronized fulfillment and monitoring of all conditions is complicated.

Moreover, reform is a continuous process. The required legislation may pass through different phases or face obstacles in the process of approval and implementation. For example, the law may have been sent to congress but left dormant by a government unwilling to engage in the inevitable horse-trading, or it may have been stopped by the opposition. In such circumstances it will not be simple for the Bank to judge the degree of compliance of the executive branch with the loan covenant. The bureaucratic entanglement will most probably heighten the vulnerability of the whole process to charged political judgments. This militates against good governance in lending programs.

Alternatively, the Bank may try to identify primary conditions (in other words, those considered essential for achieving the goals of the program) (IDB, *Two Years*, 1991), against which it will measure compliance. A multiplicity of loan objectives risks an intertwining of central and ancillary conditions and a loss of transparency. The question would be why a loose assortment of regulatory policies were lumped together in the first place.

It may be obvious why borrowers accept intricate and ambitious loan conditions, but it is less understandable why the Bank cannot establish priorities and discriminate between economically desired and politically appropriate or feasible reforms. There are lessons to be learned from the World Bank's experience (World Bank 1989; Mosley 1991). Borrowers' acceptance of unmanageable conditions is a consequence of need and is dependent on assured positive net transfers from the institution; their compliance through the life of the loan will vary according to the availability of alternative sources of finance.

question. If the legislation required is indeed an important step, can the Bank trust the executive branch's word that congress will approve it? How can fulfillment prior to disbursement be adequately measured? Worse still, it ignores the democratic process. Can the Bank preempt congressional approval?

By the end of 1991, adjustment lending, which had been set at a 25 percent ceiling under the Seventh Replenishment guidelines, had exceeded a third (see Table 6.2). The ceiling was established for the whole life of the replenishment but was found inadequate for the initial demands of Group A and B countries (IDB, *Mid-Term Report,* 1992), particularly before the surge in private capital inflows. The funds allocated for policy-based lending to Group A and B countries had been depleted even before the flow to Peru and Brazil had been allowed to start. Nevertheless, the proposal to raise the ceiling was denied, given that the biggest borrowers were gradually returning to creditworthiness. This type of operation had by 1993 reached a plateau, given the stage of the reform process in these countries and the fall in interest rates in international capital markets.

## Social Sector Lending

Before it plunged into policy-based lending, the IDB devoted a significantly higher proportion of its total lending to the social sectors than either the African or Asian Development Banks and the World Bank/IDA. Despite its higher allocation to social sectors, in terms of this share reaching the poor, it has not done as well (see Table 6.3). As reviewed in Chapter 5, the Bank has not had much success in reaching its target on low-income beneficiaries. The Bank is shifting its emphasis from an ex ante mathematical measurement of the impact of projects on beneficiaries to outlining a program of action for the dialogue with each BMC. It is expected that the poverty question will be placed on the agenda in the country programming process.

Table 6.3   Human Priorities in Multilateral Flows[a]

| Agency | Social Allocation Ratio[b] 1988–1989 | Social Priority Ratio[c] 1988–1989 | Percentage of Total Flows for Human Priorities[d] 1988–1989 |
|---|---|---|---|
| IDB (including FSO) | 27.8 | 54.4 | 15.1 |
| Asian Development Bank (including special fund) | 17.5 | 64.5 | 11.3 |
| African Development Bank/ African Development Fund | 17.5 | 47.7 | 8.3 |
| IBRD/IDA | 16.6 | 32.4 | 3.4 |

Source: Griffith-Jones et al. 1994.
Notes: a. Human priorities are defined as basic education, primary health care, safe drinking water, adequate sanitation, family planning, and nutrition.
b. Social allocation ratio is the ratio of social sector lending to total lending.
c. Social priority ratio is the ratio of social sector lending (defined as expenditure reaching the poor) to total social sector lending.
d. Reflects the proportion of total flows going to human priorities, calculated by multiplying (b) x (c).

One of the Bank's recent successes in the social sector has been the support of the emergency social fund (ESF) in Bolivia between 1986 and 1990. The ESF was created as a short-term safety net to mitigate the social costs of the 1985 adjustment program for the vulnerable segments of the population. The fund received support from the IDB ($34 million from 1986 to 1990) as well as from other international donors. It provided funds for small-scale, labor-intensive projects proposed and implemented by local NGOs. The projects financed were mostly in infrastructure; they are estimated to have created nearly 41,000 jobs and added 2 percent to the GNP level over the period. The success of the fund served as an inspiration to other countries; "in Africa alone there are over twenty social funds using the same principle of a blend of government and international funding to catalyze initiatives for the construction of development projects" (Mosley in Griffith-Jones et al. 1994). Conceived as a temporary measure, its accomplishments prompted a successor, the Social Investment Fund.

Emphasis on human resource development has been gaining ground. This emphasis reflects the perception that investments in human resources are central to reducing poverty and increasing productivity (IDB, *Economic and Social Progress in Latin America,* 1993). Since 1986, lending to the social sectors has been stepped up, especially to the highly indebted countries in Group A and the low-income Group D countries. From 1991 to 1992 the Bank nearly doubled its portfolio of social projects (see Table 6.4). Lending to social sectors in 1992 and 1993 reached nearly $3 billion, one-third of the Bank's total commitments, a share well above the recent historical average and equivalent to adjustment lending during the same period. For the Eighth Replenishment, lending for social needs, equity, and poverty reduction account for 40 percent of the total volume and 50 percent of the total number of operations. On a case-by-case basis, a share of recurrent costs of social projects will be eligible for Bank financing.

Table 6.4    IDB Portfolio of Social Projects: 1991–1993

| Sectors | 1991 No. | 1991 Amount | 1992 No. | 1992 Amount | 1993 No. | 1993 Amount | Total No. | Total Amount |
|---|---|---|---|---|---|---|---|---|
| Education | 4 | 122 | 13 | 590 | 3 | 300 | 20 | 1,012 |
| Science and Technology | 2 | 119 | 3 | 500 | — | — | 5 | 619 |
| Health | 2 | 59 | 12 | 599 | 5 | 650 | 19 | 1,308 |
| Sewerage | 6 | 490 | 11 | 1,038 | 19 | 1,622 | 36 | 3,150 |
| Urban Development | 4 | 708 | 11 | 1,164 | 3 | 99 | 18 | 1,971 |
| Others | 2 | 58 | 6 | 427 | 4 | 405 | 12 | 891 |
| Subtotal | 20 | 1,556 | 56 | 4,318 | 34 | 3,076 | 110 | 8,951 |
| Total lending | 86 | 6,675 | 125 | 10,542 | 91 | 7,990 | 302 | 25,207 |
| Percent of total | 23.3 | 23.3 | 44.8 | 41.0 | 37.4 | 38.6 | 34.8 | 33.1 |
| Average value of social projects | 77.8 | | 79.4 | | 87.1 | | 81.4 | |

*Source:* IDB, *Sectores Sociales, Marco de Referancia para la Accion, 1992–93,* 1991.

In short, the Bank is taking the initiative to "emphasize the need to incorporate all sectors of society in the process of development" (IDB, *Annual Report,* 1992, 12). This must be encouraged. During the debt crisis the uneven distribution of income was aggravated. Moreover, as public spending on health, education, and other social programs fell, most social welfare indicators deteriorated markedly. Two hundred million people live in poverty in the region today, 2.5 percent over the level calculated as recently as 1986 (IDB/UNDP, *Social Reform and Poverty,* 1993).

The Bank is committed to implementing institutional reforms for the scope and delivery of social services by highlighting social issues in the programming process and country dialogue. It can also enhance poverty reduction through careful selection and design of projects, including improved targeting of benefits to the poor. As part of this process, it has joined forces with the UNDP to promote a consensus on the urgency of social reform. This collaboration produced *Social Reform and Poverty,* which was discussed at a meeting of regional leaders in February 1993. The exercise was intended to identify a set of principles for public policy and social reform to start a dialogue and programming process with the BMCs.

The president has also established a social agenda policy group chaired by Louis Emmerij. The group established priorities for the social agenda and coordinated these with the macroeconomic reforms under way. Three pilot case studies were undertaken in Chile, Trinidad and Tobago, and Venezuela; a fourth one was due to be undertaken in Costa Rica in 1994. As a result of these preliminary studies, a new window has been proposed to lend to social sectors in tandem with policy loans to create the appropriate policy, institutional, and organizational setting. The new window would be open to countries when they undertake a socioeconomic reform package. It would have an "active" policy lending arm that would prepare the ground for the "passive" investment arm. Once the reforms are in place, the Bank would continue to fund traditional investment projects. The approach is still under discussion. Some countries are concerned after the experiences of previous policy loans in relation to the multiplicity and proliferation of policy targets and the administrative burden put on a weakened public sector that might make loans unmanageable (for example, in Argentina). Others are reluctant to increase their external indebtedness on ordinary capital terms (such as Costa Rica and Chile).

Sustainability of a project means that it must generate enough funds for implementation and operation. The financial sustainability of externally funded social sector projects that do not generate an income stream concerns many BMCs. Recurrent costs tend to be underfunded in many BMCs, partly because of lack of adequate tax policies, the lack of user fees, and the greater political dividends obtained from new projects in comparison with the maintenance of old projects. The dilemma for poverty reduction is that human capital investments require considerable financing of recurrent costs. Proponents of externally funded investments in human capital argue that these are more productive than investment in physical capital (World Bank 1990, 86). Critics of this approach counter that recurrent costs tend to loom large in overall budgets. An additional concern is that, if the government cannot currently fund recurrent costs, how will it be able to generate future recurrent costs and the foreign exchange to service the debt? (World Bank, *Poverty Reduction*, 1992.) A possibility now under consideration at the IDB is an extension of grace and maturity periods for these loans. In addition, the Bank will need to consider a financial framework for the sector tied to the country's fiscal policies. Provisions for ensuring sustainability after support from the Bank ends should also be considered. Although the leverage of the Bank will be reduced at that point, performance on sustaining past projects could be made a condition of future support.

Some innovative programs are taking into account the institutional circumstances in the BMCs. Modeled on the World Bank's Economic Development Institute, a teaching center to train "social managers" is planned.

A four-year pilot program for youth training in Chile has received attention from other BMCs. The program, designed to reduce youth unemployment, rests only marginally on governmental institutions. Its goal is to provide training for 100,000 young people. The program targets fifteen- to twenty-four-year-old people in low-income families who are not enrolled in formal schooling. Educational institutes compete for the design and implementation of courses through an open bidding process. Part of the training provided must be on the job so that links between the demands of the private sector and the skills of the target population are developed and strengthened. Selection of educational institutes is based on the quality and price of the course offered and on the number of trainees for whom on-the-job training is guaranteed. To target entrants into the labor market, only a small grant is awarded—less than a third of the minimum wage during class period, with slightly higher levels when trainees enter firms.

## Regional Leadership

With the increase in lending brought about by the Seventh Replenishment, the Bank's presence in the region also increased. In 1991, the Bank resumed its traditional role as the major source of multilateral financing to the region (see Figure 6.1). This was most evident in Group A and B countries where the decline had been greatest and where the IDB took advantage of the World Bank's prior pipeline. Still, to its Group C and D countries, the IDB provides one and a half to two times the volume of assistance provided by the World Bank (see Figure 6.1).

The IDB has also been the major source of technical assistance for the region, a key component of intellectual leadership. This program falls into three main categories. The first is technical assistance tied to specific projects; it covers preinvestment and assistance in project execution, including the creation or strengthening of institutions. The second category consists of special studies and promotional activities. The third category comprises training projects and programs carried out by the IDB. Together with the UNDP, it has financed the Instituto Latinoamericano de Planificacion Economica y Social (ILPES) in Santiago, which provided training courses in economic and social development. It assisted governments in preparing plans and programs and in gathering adequate statistics. The Bank today is venturing into new frontiers for technical assistance by designing programs for the modernization of legislatures and the judiciary.

Nonreimbursable technical assistance, which is crucial to increase the absorptive capacity of Group D countries, is mostly financed from the net income of the FSO.[8] It is projected to dwindle in future years—a shortfall that may be covered by a special fund, FONTEC, which has been proposed as a result of the Eighth Replenishment. FONTEC should not only preserve this key function of the Bank but also help to consolidate funds obtained from bilateral sources, increase transparency in the use of funds, and focus hitherto fragmented technical cooperation.

The Bank now plays an important role in overall hemispheric relations. It has been an active proponent and the "key facilitator" of the EAI (IDB, *Annual Report*, 1990, 5). It has financed an analysis of Western Hemisphere free trade for all the countries concerned and sponsored a series of colloquia and conferences. It has a hand in the support of economic integration, notably in Central America, the Caribbean, the Andean Group, and the Southern Cone; and it contributes to studies on the improvement of physical integration through the Parana-Paraguay Waterway (the longest inland seaway in the world), the Buenos Aires–São Paulo highway, the project to integrate railway systems in the Southern Cone, the project to link up electric power grid systems in Central America, and so on.

In addition, the president is working on the severe social problems that beset the region. In his speech to the 1992 Annual Meeting, Enrique Iglesias identified two major regional tasks "crucial to the viability of the development model being applied today by the countries of Latin America. First and most urgent, is to reduce extreme poverty through appropriate countermeasures. Second, is to move towards a more integrated society."

The Bank's maintenance of an intellectual dialogue on the social aspects of development is exemplified by a debate over a strategy toward Peru during the administration of Alan García. Then manager of the economic and social department, Miguel Urrutia, and J. Levinson, general counsel, emphasized that continued lending could help prevent further deterioration of social conditions. They questioned whether it was wise to cut off all financing because of poor performance and argued for continued selective assistance to support basic services such as potable water and sewerage. "To put the point negatively the IDB was not established to replicate the role of the IMF. Neither was it intended that it should be a refinancing agency for commercial debt" (Please 1989, 2–3).

The IDB retained its individuality by being in touch with the problems of the region and one step ahead of the policymakers. Working with the UNDP, the Bank called together a group of statesmen, scientists, and experts to reflect on the problems of sustainable development. *Our Own Agenda* was written by the Latin American and Caribbean Commission on Development and the Environment to mobilize public opinion in Latin America and encourage participation in the 1992 Earth Summit in Rio. *Amazonia without Myths* was a similar effort by the Commission on Development and the Environment for Amazonia to focus on the Amazon region.

In addition, the Bank has created a program to tap the intellectual and research potential in the region to plan economic and social policies. A network of regional institutes in applied economics do research on policy-relevant questions. The themes so far have included timing and sequencing of trade liberalization, privatization, liberalization, productivity and economic development, savings and investment, the public sector and income distribution, external shocks, and stabilization policies. While the intellectual returns of the program are considerable, its budgetary impact is small; it is supported by a $4.7 million nonreimbursable, regional technical cooperation grant from the FSO. Gradually, urgency should give way to issues of sustainability, and the network can contribute to a long-term development agenda.

Stanley Please (1989), one of the architects of structural adjustment loans at the World Bank, argued strongly against IDB involvement in adjustment lending to directly productive sectors on the grounds that the major policy issues for these sectors relate to trade and exchange rate policy. Given the lead of the IMF in exchange rate policy and the advantage of the World Bank in trade, he suggested that the IDB could be either a passive collaborator in the negotiation, or it would create divisiveness within the multilateral institutions, a situation "in which, to be frank, it is unlikely to have much impact on the final outcome" (Please 1989, 13). He advocated that the IDB retain its comparative advantage in infrastructure and socioeconomic sectors. These are issues to which the IMF has paid little attention, and to which the World Bank has paid far less attention than it has to trade policy.

Even if one were to cede pluralism for the sake of efficiency, this division of labor would be possible only in countries in which there is both a Fund and a World Bank program in place. Furthermore, the IDB cannot avoid trade policy. True, it need not duplicate the World Bank's expertise in trade liberalization; indeed it would be difficult to catch up on twenty years of research. But trade policy cannot be ignored at a time of activism in regional integration and when the merits of "governing the market" are gaining ground (Wade 1990). Indeed, although there is consensus about the superiority of an outward-oriented trade policy, much disagreement still remains on subsidiary issues: the sequencing and timing of reform, the level and dismantling of trade barriers, the extent of overall (and sectoral) protection, and the pace of reform as a whole. The work of Krueger has neither invalidated the argument for protecting infant industries nor established that the success of Korea and Taiwan was based on a strategy of laissez faire. "The [World] Bank's efforts at trade policy reform constitute for this reason one of the most controversial elements of its proposed reform programmes" (Mosley 1991, 94).

The IDB should involve itself at this stage in assistance to trade policy. It must help BMCs increase their institutional and technological capabilities to promote development and access to markets through a creative private sector/public sector relationship. It must look at the institutions affecting trade and the financing mechanisms. The Bank's expertise must not be restricted to an in-house buildup of skills. Policy analysis skills must be supported where they are most needed—in the BMCs.

The IDB should also help countries with the compatibility and consistency of the integration schemes now growing in a haphazard way. Much of the flurry of trade-related activism in the region was prompted by U.S. president Bush's call for a free trade area covering the whole Western Hemisphere. Some of the optimism it generated is not warranted. Even if the free trade area were to meet the time schedules set at the 1994 Hemisphere Summit, it would not guarantee sustained economic progress. While the agenda of hemispheric integration takes shape, more immediate tasks await. The Bank must increase its analytical capacity in the area of anticipated economic adjustments and must be prepared to support adjustment assistance. Attention must be paid to the potential losers when free trade alters patterns of production and employment. The Bank must ensure coherence of regional free trade with its social agenda and with the antipoverty efforts of recipients, so that the historical difficulties of reaching low-income beneficiaries are not repeated. Bottlenecks in regional physical infrastructure (ports, roads, communications, and so forth) are good candidates for IDB involvement in the immediate future. The IDB has both the appropriate staff and field representation to handle these needs.

Up until the present, adjustment lending has only marginally followed a pattern in which the respective expertise of the IDB and the World Bank were balanced. U.S. mistrust of a borrower-controlled bank drove the IDB into reliance on the World Bank pipeline and thus imposed limits on Bank contributions. As Bank expertise grows and as the countries in the region reduce price distortions, public expenditure will need to be restructured to maintain social services and to ensure that projects are sustainable. New investments must be generated, and new institutions and regulatory frameworks must be designed. It has been calculated that the cost of building a hospital is equivalent to about three subsequent years of recurrent costs. Health policy must consider both aspects, and governments need assistance in planning both systems because they have a natural inclination for the "ribbon-cutting syndrome"—a preference for new projects with a high profile and political rewards, particularly at election time. As in the 1960s, when the IDB cooperated in setting up national accounting practices, an emphasis such as this would require improved technical cooperation to support policy implementation and the development of institutional capabilities. Public sector managers must be trained, despite the low salaries and low availability of qualified technical staff in the public sector.

The IDB can follow the focus of IMF–World Bank macro programs and at the same time place emphasis on the distributional impact of public spending cuts. To consolidate its campaign on social development and poverty alleviation, it should ensure consistency of these goals with those of other IFIs. It must accompany its BMCs in the drawing of the Policy Framework Papers (PFPs). It is crucial that the IDB, via policy dialogue, discover ways in which governments can allocate a higher share of their budget to social expenditures, thus improving the structure of government spending. It is also important that the level of government spending be considered; tax reforms and effective collection systems will have to be envisioned as an integral part of the poverty reduction strategy.

The IDB's advantage lies in its degree of specialization and its ability to respond to local conditions. IDB field offices can maintain an especially close relationship and rapport with BMCs. Field offices can identify projects; their representatives are a channel for continuous communications between the Bank and the local implementers of the projects. Given the Bank's contact with local conditions, it has an a priori strategic advantage over the World Bank. Yet more use could be made of this asset.

Field office staff oversee the execution of loan clauses because disbursement procedures require that countries submit all invoices to the Bank. Operational procedures need to be greatly simplified. More delegation of responsibilities at all levels from the Board downwards is required. The IDB's field office specialists, once relieved of cumbersome minutiae, could take a more active role in helping executing agencies solve problems during project implementation. "Field Office specialists think that too many issues must be decided by the Operations Division in HQs; Operations staff think that too many matters have to be decided by the Board" (IDB, *Evaluation Report*, 1990, 9). While a substantial amount of delegation has been made since this report was issued, additional delegation should be made. It could lead to further improvements in project execution and to more grassroots initiatives. The satisfactory operation of an evaluation unit may make delegation politically acceptable in the future. Hand in hand with decentralization, the Bank must supply the skills mix needed by field offices to proceed with the new regional agenda.

The regional community includes other organizations beyond the IDB. The Organization of American States and the Economic Commission for Latin America and the Caribbean are two of the major players whose roles are currently being reassessed. These three institutions are the tripod on which hemispheric integration will rest. While a reduced ECLAC remains committed to the realm of research, analysis, and technical assistance, former president, Cesar Gaviria of Colombia, newly elected secretary general of the OAS, plans to restore a renewed sense of mission. The countries of the region are committed to the OAS and have assigned it the lead in organizing responses to any democratic breakdown.

The OAS member states did react to the breakdown of constitutional rule in Haiti in 1991 and in Peru in 1992. In the case of Peru, the IDB blocked the disbursement of loans already approved by the Board until President Fujimori promised a return to constitutional rule. The OAS still does not have an agreed operational strategy for confronting democratic breakdowns, but in the meantime the IDB could bolster constitutional democracy by requiring that military expenditures be directed by elected civilian authorities and that their impact be incorporated into fiscal policy goals. This will be a slow and sensitive process in many countries. In the meantime, the IDB's initiatives to strengthen legislatures and judicial systems are an important step toward the attainment of good governance.

## Notes

1. In some cases, as in Argentina, where the military was in principle opposed to such planning, President Frondizi's civilian government of the time had to undertake the commitment discreetly to avoid upsetting political sensitivities.

2. Had it not been able to convince the IMF, it would have had to follow the IMF's judgment or not go forward with the loan.

3. The PFP is a policy document drafted by the Fund and amended and agreed upon by the World Bank and the borrowing government. It sets out the understandings on the economic situation of the country and the necessary remedial policies. At present it is used only in very poor borrowing countries. It is a prerequisite for access to the Structural Adjustment Facility (SAF) and the Enhanced Structural Adjustment Facility (ESAF) at the Fund.

4. This trend is not applicable since 1988 during which lending concentrated on the higher income countries because of the weight of policy loans in the overall lending program. The bigger debtors moved more quickly into sectoral adjustment; moreover, the IDB was required to cofinance such loans with the World Bank, so its lending program became biased toward World Bank priorities. As sector lending has reached its peak, the temporary trend may soon be reversed.

5. Interviews with IDB staff.

6. Mosley also proposed lending directly to the microentrepreneurs themselves, a possibility for which the Bank does not have the expertise, nor is it cost effective to take on a multitude of such small-scale operations.

7. Consultants are used to prepare private sector diagnostics to identify constraints on private sector investment; these diagnostics are the foundation of the investment sector loans described in this chapter.

8. Bilateral sources have helped to finance technical cooperation. A prominent example is the Japanese Fund, which finances around 20 percent of total commitments.

# 7

# Resource Mobilization and Portfolio Management

This chapter describes trends in resource flows and the quality of the loan portfolio before reviewing the contribution of the Bank to the region's recovery. In a subsequent section concessional funds are addressed. The chapter ends with a review of operational efficiency.

The debt crisis in the 1980s altered the role of all IFIs in the region. The crisis was diagnosed as a temporary liquidity problem, and, before a proper debt strategy was in place, the IDB played a vital compensatory role, as the country studies of Costa Rica, Bolivia, and Argentina show. Under the Sixth Replenishment in 1982–1986 (before the Bank was brought to a standstill over disagreement for the terms of the Seventh Replenishment), it managed to deliver positive net transfers[1] to the region. As a "loyal, bad weather friend" (Griffith-Jones et al. 1994), this expedient was valuable at a time of overall massive negative transfers.

However, the lead in formulating the debt strategy after 1985 was handed to the Bretton Woods institutions. Between 1985 and 1988 the strategy relied on the Baker Plan based on a combination of growth, structural adjustment, and new flows. Yet the new lending did not materialize as expected, and many debtor countries faced increasingly negative net transfers to IFIs, including the IDB, after 1986. Belatedly, the IDB began to actively ease the regional financing gap once the Seventh Replenishment was put into place in 1989. By that time the Baker Plan was threadbare. The Brady Plan replaced it with a proposal that countries with sound adjustment programs should obtain access to debt and debt service reduction facilities (DDSR) supported by the Fund, the World Bank, and the IDB.

## Resource Flows

The IDB has been an active generator of resource transfers to its BMCs. Since inception until the last general resource increase in 1994, it operated in four-year funding cycles. At the end of each period subscribed capital (paid-in and callable) was replenished. Paid-in capital amounted to $3.1 billion at the end of 1993, but cumulative subscriptions to its ordinary capital were nearly twenty times larger as a result of the unpaid callable subscriptions. The paid-in ratios have declined with each replenishment, and the Bank has relied increasingly on its borrowings in international capital markets against its capital base. Thanks to this backing, it was able to lend a total of $63 billion during the thirty-three years of operations up to 1993. The volume of total investment in projects financed with the help of the Bank was estimated at $170 billion (IDB, *Annual Report*, 1993).

The start of the Seventh Replenishment coincided with a decline in interest rates in the United States to the lowest level in thirty years. This provided a positive external shock to BMCs, and a new period of access to financial inflows was inaugurated. In 1993 private capital inflows totaled $60 billion, 77 percent over the level reached in 1992 and three and a half times larger than the one in 1990. The positive shock allowed a resumption of growth but has also complicated the management of economic policy by appreciating exchange rates, increasing reserves, and swelling money supply throughout the region.

The IDB has always worked with preset guidelines for allocation of resources among country groups. These were set at the Bank's inception when financial markets were stable and stringent to allow a fair distribution of resources among countries with varying absorptive capacities. To ensure access to resources for the small countries in Groups C and D, a 65 percent cap was established for Groups A and B under the Seventh Replenishment. It has been retained over the life of the Eighth Replenishment. Lending to Groups C and D is supported by technical assistance in project preparation. In addition, they are also granted a higher share of foreign exchange financing. Allowable foreign exchange financing shares are 50 percent for Group A countries, 60 percent for Group B countries, 40 percent for Group C countries, and 80 percent for Group D countries.

The Seventh Replenishment allowed the Bank to project a $22.5 billion lending program in 1990–1993. New lending guidelines, together with a change of management and a renewed sense of mission, resulted in a hike in lending volumes. Commitments began to beat yearly records, growing by about $1 billion a year in 1990, 1991, and 1992. In 1990–1993, actual loan commitments reached $21.1 billion.

These volumes were concentrated in the Group A and B countries. Nevertheless, commitments increased at a greater rate for the smaller C and D countries than for the A and B countries. The figures also show that the IDB still lends more than the World Bank in the C and D countries.

Gross loan disbursements were boosted by the large share of fast-disbursing loans. In 1991 gross disbursements reached $3.1 billion, an increase of 33 percent over the previous year. In 1992 disbursements managed a slight increase, and in 1993 they reached nearly $3.8 billion. Net disbursements (disbursements less loan repayments) also increased. They reached $1 billion in 1990 and peaked at $1.6 billion in 1993, to reach over a third of total official flows to the region (IDB, *Annual Report*, 1993).

The magnitude of disbursements after the initial improvement of the cash flow situation of BMCs might have created serious aggregate negative flows in the medium term. The Bank's study, *Two Years of Sector Lending Operations Cofinanced with the World Bank* (1991), warned that by 1995 the dynamics of adjustment operations could impose a burden on countries' cash flow when repayments become due. Serious negative net transfers toward the end of the decade could, in turn, exercise pressure on the Bank to maintain a continuous flow of large fast-disbursing operations (IDB, *Two Years*, 1991, 19).

However, two developments have altered the nature of the problem. First and most important, the massive inflow of private capital into the region since 1991 has reversed the trend and led to a situation of almost overabundance of foreign exchange reserves in many countries; among them are three of the four largest IDB borrowers, Mexico, Chile, and Argentina. The Bank and all IFIs have been fortunate that such large private inflows have helped to compensate for their growing negative net transfers. The pressure on the IDB to maintain a self-sustaining flow of positive transfers has been lifted. Countries can now repay their growing shares of multilateral debt comfortably. Indeed, a case can be made for the BMCs to accelerate their repayments and relieve the upward pressure on exchange rates confronting them, even if inflows may not remain constant at present levels. Repayments could be brought forward by granting BMCs special temporary incentives.

Second, the pace of disbursements, although on the rise in 1993, has been somewhat slower after the first tranche than expected. Poor public management and weak institutional development in the BMCs impaired the disbursement record. Some of the problems in disbursements can also be traced to the proliferation of policy targets and the intricate design of the loans themselves, which led to cumbersome management and difficulties in implementation. The implementation of some of these loans has been so complicated and has involved so many agents as to conspire against speed in disbursing, as in the case of Argentina.

The increase in lending volumes was not reflected in positive net transfers. BMCs have become net exporters of capital to the Bank since 1990, as they were in 1987–1988. As can be seen in Table 7.1, there has been only a brief reprieve in 1989 when disbursements actually exceeded debt service. (Disbursements picked up with the Seventh Replenishment, due to an increase in interest payments on past loans.) World Bank transfers to the region also turned negative in 1987 and on a far larger scale than the IDB's, reaching $2.6 billion in 1991.

As the main debtor countries return to creditworthiness, the urgency of speedy disbursements has decreased. Chile, for example, has put disbursements on a slower track to lessen massive inflows of foreign exchange. Other countries, though not confronting such over-flow, are still less constrained in foreign exchange than they were in the 1980s. The IDB began to act countercyclically and slow down its fast-disbursing programs in countries with improved balance-of-payments positions.

The Bank's increased lending resulted in an increased share in the region's external debt, growing from 3.6 percent in 1985 to 5.8 percent in 1992. In comparison, the IDB's share in total multilateral debt has fallen from 45.6 percent to 40.9 percent over the same period, although it is projected to grow in the second half of the 1990s as the slowdown in World Bank commitments in the early 1990s becomes tangible.

Since the beginning of 1994, and at the time of writing, U.S. interest rates have begun to rise. Negative transfers could again wreak havoc on the payments position of BMCs should the trend continue. Given the region's sensitivity to changes in G-7 monetary policies and the IDB's need to safeguard its own portfolio and to provide BMCs with adequate assistance, the Bank should build up its analytical capabilities to anticipate the consequences of these fluctuations. Coupled with country-risk analysis, this would enable the Bank to be more responsive to the changing circumstances of BMCs than is possible under preset country allocations. Preset country allocations are a legacy of stable capital markets and scarce funding alternatives; they served to distribute resources in a cooperative spirit, but more flexibility is required to cope with volatile capital markets and the financial liberalization undertaken by BMCs.

## IDB's Portfolio

Seventy percent of the Bank's disbursed loans are concentrated in six countries: Brazil, Mexico, Argentina, Colombia, Chile, and Peru. It

Table 7.1  IDB Net Flows and Net Transfers to Latin American Countries: 1982–1992 (U.S.$ millions)

| | 1982 | 1983 | 1984 | 1985 | 1986 | 1987 | 1988 | 1989 | 1990 | 1991 | 1992 |
|---|---|---|---|---|---|---|---|---|---|---|---|
| IDB net flows | 1,182 | 1,217 | 1,787 | 1,700 | 1,484 | 990 | 1,168 | 1,327 | 1,132 | 1,263 | -465 |
| IDB net transfers | 678 | 707 | 1,186 | 929 | 499 | -155 | -23 | 24 | -276 | -296 | -196 |
| Total net transfers | -11,200 | -24,800 | -14,400 | -26,900 | -23,400 | -14,400 | -24,100 | -24,200 | -11,800 | -7,400 | 11,500 |
| World Bank net transfers | 562 | 788 | 1,048 | 771 | 1,031 | -508 | -838 | -1,145 | 291 | -2,630 | — |

Sources: IDB data base; World Bank, World Debt Tables 1992–1993, in Griffith-Jones et al. 1994.

must be remembered that these countries account for over 85 percent of the region's GNP and seem to moving out of their payments crises. Exposure in Argentina is expected to reach a modest level of 4.8 percent of total external debt by 1995 and in Mexico, 1.4 percent. The Bank does not have criteria for creditworthiness nor a graduation policy. The only mechanism to contain the risk of overconcentration of the Bank's portfolio in the countries with greatest absorptive capacity (Argentina, Brazil, Mexico, and Venezuela) lies in the allocation guidelines by country groups that are established at each replenishment.

However, the risk to the IDB's portfolio stems less from loan concentration than from high exposure in the small, severely indebted low-income countries. A feature of the debt crisis of the 1980s was a buildup of arrears of principal and interest on loans. Although the biggest borrowers managed to avoid arrears over one hundred and eighty days, protracted arrears were concentrated in a few small countries, namely Nicaragua, Honduras, Peru, and Panama. Loans to Guyana were never nonperforming, although the country was declared ineligible by the IMF in 1985.

Many countries had to fall into arrears despite knowing the preferred creditor status of the IDB and its policy not to participate in reschedulings. Thus, a share of the Bank's loans was in nonaccrual status from 1987 until 1992. This share peaked at 8 percent of loans outstanding in 1989. Honduras became current in 1990, and, as a result, nonaccruals outstanding fell to 6.1 percent. As regional performance revived, loan repayments improved significantly since 1991 when Peru, the fifth largest borrower, and Nicaragua cleared their arrears. In 1991 Peru returned to borrowing from the IDB after six years of virtual exclusion. At that point the IDB took the lead in an international rescue package with a credit of $640 million. When Panama became current in 1992 the Bank was clear of loans in nonaccrual status.[2]

The Bank's conservative financial policies reduce the risk associated with a loan portfolio with potential servicing problems.[3] For example, the IDB's sanctions policy requires that, when arrears exceed thirty days, loans disbursements to the borrower are suspended; after one hundred and twenty days new loan proposals for the country are not considered; and after one hundred and eighty days all loans to the country are placed in nonaccrual status, although management can postpone this sanction if there is a perception of forthcoming collectability.

The Bank began to provision for loan losses in 1988, when its loans on nonaccrual status as a share of loans outstanding reached 2.6 percent. Provisions were made against specific loans after they had fallen into nonaccrual status. Monthly provisions were made based upon an amount equivalent to one-twelfth of 10 percent of the outstanding loan balance in nonaccrual status, which would approximate a yearly provision of 10 percent of the nonaccruing loan balance. The loan-loss policy shifted to general provisioning in 1991 to allow a margin for shock. To take into consideration the general collectibility risk of the portfolio, the new policy provides that the Bank maintain a target loan-loss provisioning allowance of 3 percent of outstanding loans. (By way of comparison the level maintained by the World Bank is 2.5 percent.) Loan-loss provisions nearly reached the target by the end of 1992.

A recurrence of debt-servicing problems could flare up in the severely indebted low-income countries, as defined by the World Bank, which on average show debt-to-GDP ratios of 100 percent and debt-to-exports ratios of 441 percent. Nicaragua's debt-to-GDP ratio stands at over 600 percent, and its debt-to-exports ratio is 3,000 percent. The possibility of chronic arrears requiring a bailout cannot be discounted. Bolivia, Honduras, Nicaragua, and Guyana also depend heavily on multilateral concessional financing and, after the Eighth Replenishment, are expected to borrow only on concessional terms or on humanitarian grounds. Steps may be taken to reduce the risk of overexposure to the Bank. In Bolivia, IDB exposure stands at 29 percent of external debt, in Jamaica at 11 percent, and in Honduras at 15 percent. In the last two countries the overall ratio of debt service to exports stands at a critical 27 percent, and the Bank's exposure is expected to reach between 50 and 60 percent of total multilateral exposure by 1995. In Costa Rica and Panama it stood at 41 percent in 1992.

The Bank's risk could be lessened by reshuffling the composition of the country groups according to debt indicators. If Jamaica were placed in Group D instead of C, Jamaica might have greater access to concessional terms or to a softer blend of resources. Moving Peru from Group B into Group C would also reduce the Bank's risk. The move would be strongly resisted by C countries, which would either have to share resources in a different manner or be selected for graduation out of Group C. A country-risk analysis unit should be set up to anticipate servicing difficulties and design lending according to the respective debt profiles, particularly of severely indebted low-income countries to which the Bank is most exposed and that have meager alternative funding.

The Bank does not have a policy of graduating borrowers completely—that is, terminating their access to all Bank loans. Country-risk analysis could allow for appropriate policies on flexible graduation. The application of a graduation policy for its top four BMCs could free resources, but it would also weaken the Bank's portfolio because those borrowers are its most creditworthy. It could be argued that this could undermine its triple-A credit rating and lead to an increase in interest rates charged to the remaining borrowers. It is difficult to determine how capital markets would react to a change in the composition of the portfolio. Protection against default is ultimately given by the uncalled capital committed by donor countries, particularly the United States, so in the short run the risk of bondholders would not change. In the long term, none of the donor members is likely to countenance a call on its capital. However, temporary graduation or withdrawal from active borrowing, as in the case of Venezuela during its 1970s oil bonanza, would not significantly alter the quality of the portfolio and could release resources for countries with severe debt problems.

## Participation of the IDB in the Region's Recovery

The hike in lending volumes from the IDB coincided with a recovery of the region's economic performance. After the years of decline and depression, growth in the region began to pick up at the beginning of the 1990s (see Figure 7.1). New conditions in international financial markets and the massive increase in private capital flows played a major role in the recovery. The process has had a dynamism of its own, which is nurtured by the Bank.

Figure 7.1    Latin America: Growth and Inflation, 1984–1992 (in percent)

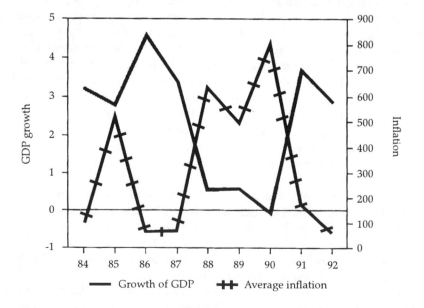

Source: IDB, "Ecomonic and Social Progress in Latin America," 1993 Report, 3.

The IDB has supported its BMCs in their recovery mainly by providing fast-disbursing resources on a sector basis and through loans to reduce debt and debt service. In contrast to the World Bank macroeconomic approach to SECALs, the IDB chose this type of loan because of its previous expertise in sector-based adjustment operations.

One of the critical factors affecting resource mobilization is the effectiveness of the organization in putting countries on the track of economic policy reform. The influence of the Bank has been significant in qualitative terms because of its attack on fiscal imbalances, the strategic direction imparted on lending, and an improved dialogue with BMCs.

In quantitative terms, a key factor contributing to creditworthiness in the region has been the reduction of the external debt burden. The IDB did not participate in the first Brady deals put together for Mexico and Venezuela; it became active in DDSR schemes only in 1992. The participation of the Bank in such operations was approved by the Board of Governors in October 1990. A DDSR facility was established as an integral part of the Bank's fast-disbursing program. The operational guidelines restrict the IDB's participation to cofinancing the overall program with the World Bank (IDB, *Debt and Debt Service,* 1991).

The most comprehensive debt-related operation in which the IDB has participated to date is the one for Argentina. The DDSR loan played a central part in Argentina's overall lending program. The reduction of the debt overhang contributed to improvement of the underlying conditions for macroeconomic stability and for the establishment of a medium-term development strategy. The loan itself is linked to the fiscal framework of the government's recovery program, which attacked the overall public sector deficit, including those of local governments. The single tranche loan was fully disbursed after the debt reduction agreement between the private banks and the government was finalized. IDB, World Bank, and IMF funds were disbursed simultaneously.

The DDSR loan has contributed to the restructuring of all medium- and long-term commercial debt amounting to some $20.9 billion (about half of Argentina's public and publicly guaranteed debt) and approximately $8.3 billion on past due interest. The reduction was applied only to the outstanding principal while past due interest was settled by a partial down payment of $700 million and an exchange of the remainder for par bonds bearing market interest rates. The debt reduction amounted to about $11 billion or 38 percent of public debt with commercial banks. However, Argentina needed to borrow more than $2 billion from official sources; so, in effect, the debt burden has been reduced by less than $9 billion or 15 percent of total public external debt (commercial banks plus all other sources). These results are similar to those obtained in the Mexican DDSR agreement. Despite these reduced figures, the operation contributed to settling accounts with external private creditors.

The participation of the IDB (and other IFIs) in debt reduction has turned debt owed to private creditors that might be rescheduled into fixed liabilities owed to creditors that do not reschedule. In the long term, flexibility in debt management has been reduced. Moreover, the IDB's exposure to Argentina as a result of the entire loan package increased from its historical share of 2 percent to 4 percent. Argentina was the country to which the Bank made the largest volume of loan commitments in 1992 and 1993. So far the Bank has been fortunate that its own risk has been tempered by the overall improvement in Argentina's external solvency indicators, thanks mainly to the revival of international private flows. There was an improvement in investment ratios after the operation, but cause and effect cannot be demonstrated. Argentina's own massive debt conversion/privatization program has also made a significant contribution by trimming public debt (both external and domestic) by approximately $12 billion. The IDB participated in this program by charting the restructuring of the national and provincial power utilities.

In short, the quantitative contribution of the IDB has been significant, but it is difficult to isolate from the reversal of overall net transfers to the region. Countries that did not undertake policy reforms or undertook them only partially enjoyed a turn-around in their inflows as well (Calvo et al. 1993).

The qualitative contribution has posed other difficulties. A third of the Bank's total policy-based lending in the 1990 to early 1993 period was for reform of the financial sector or for reform of investment policies. (The list of adjustment loans with a financial sector component can be found in Table 7.2.) The purpose of these operations was to foster efficiency in financial markets so that, on the one hand, domestic savings were channeled into productive long-term investments, and, on the other, capital inflows into BMCs are sustained. The range of reforms includes removing entry restrictions, improving the supervision of banks and securities markets, liberalizing credit and interest rates, privatization, and restructuring of DFIs. Legal and regulatory reform are included, particularly in second and third tranches. Over and above conditionality, the IDB has also provided technical assistance in this area. In Mexico, for example, it assisted the Securities Exchange Commission in establishing a second-tier stock market (Griffith-Jones et al. 1994).

Conditionality is a sensitive instrument to be used with caution. At times some conditionalities have been redundant, while at other times they have aroused bitter controversies. The debate on government-

Table 7.2    Sector Loans with a Financial Sector Component

| Country | Type Loan | Year | IDB Loan Amount (U.S.$ millions) | Comments |
|---|---|---|---|---|
| Venezuela | FSL[a] | 1990 | | First financial sector loan |
| Chile | ISL[b] | 1991 | 150.0 | First ISL |
| Bolivia | FSL/ISL | 1991 | 60.0 | Tied to multisectoral credit (MSC) |
| Uruguay | FSL | 1991 | 152.0 | Followed by MSC in 1992 |
| Nicaragua | T&F[c] | 1991 | 133.0 | |
| Colombia | ISL | 1991 | 205.0 | Will be followed by MSC in 1993 |
| Peru | FSL | 1992 | 221.8 | Certain reforms required before can develop an MSC |
| Uruguay | ISL | 1992 | 65.0 | Emphasis on capital markets, especially the development of contractual savings. Linked conceptually to MSC |
| El Salvador | ISL | 1992 | 90.0 | Improves the basic conditions for the existing MSC, especially prudential regulation |
| Argentina | ISl | 1992 | 350.0 | Emphasis on prudential regulation and resolving the problems of the provincial banks. Will be followed with MSC in 1993 |
| Paraguay | ISl | 1992 | 70.0 | Deals with the most fundamental issues for the development of financial institutions and contractual savings |
| Costa Rica | ISL | 1992 | 100.0 | Cross-conditionality with parallel MSC |

*Source:* Griffith-Jones et al. 1994.
*Notes:* a. Financial sector loan.
b. Investment sector loan.
c. Trade and finance.

induced distortions in the economy is far from closed, and a fresh look is due in Latin America before many policy reforms are included in the conditionality packages. More policy analysis capacity must be built before the Bank gives policy advice to BMCs. For example, the protection of intellectual property rights as part of investment sector loans is debatable. Economic theory has not been able to prove that such protection provides a stimulus to foreign private investment to BMCs, nor that it stimulates indigenous technological capabilities. The adverse consequences for developing countries include higher royalty payments to foreign innovators, a corresponding loss of investment opportunities in domestic research and development, higher prices for products under monopoly rights, and greater dependence on imports in general. "On the bleakest view, a developing country stands to gain only when a foreign invention affords solutions of particular local utility that would not otherwise obtain sufficient investment in research and development" (Reichman 1993, 5).

The Bank could use the network of research institutes that it has supported with a grant from the FSO to improve the quality of its policy advice. It should commission analyses on the Bank's agenda and should integrate the results of this research into the design of future loans.

## Mobilization of Concessional Resources

An advantage of being in the U.S. sphere of influence during the Cold War was that Latin America had a strong claim on U.S. transfers for the launching of the IDB's Fund for Special Operations in 1959. But concessional funds have become scarce both in relative and absolute terms. In 1975 at the Fourth Replenishment they were restricted to Groups C and D. In 1983 at the Sixth Replenishment there was a further limitation: Group D countries became the only countries eligible for foreign exchange lending from FSO resources. The Intermediate Financing Facility was created to provide some element of concessionality by subsidizing the interest on lending from ordinary capital resources. Allocation of IFF resources allowed approximately 60 percent for Group C and 40 percent for Group D countries.

The Seventh Replenishment in 1989 allocated nearly $900 million of IFF lending to the Group C countries, and $240 million of IFF and all FSO lending was to go to Group D countries. Although the state of many BMCs required considerable access to concessional resources, only $200 million was raised in the form of new contributions. As a result, nearly all the concessional resources required to achieve a $1.86 billion lending program had to be generated internally by the Bank. The IFF was to be funded by annual transfers from FSO reserves mandated through the year 2010. For the FSO, $1.66 billion in commitments for 1990–1993 was made against loan repayments expected over the 1994–1997 period. In short, the Bank funded the bulk of the concessional lending program by committing most of its projected future reflows and income. The combined FSO and IFF lending of about $2 billion was still not sufficient to meet the financing needs of Group D countries, which had to borrow from ordinary capital resources.

Group D countries have some of the poorest debt indicators. They face decreasing bilateral lending; little or no growth in World Bank funding, including from IDA; and meager prospects of private sources of financing. Given the economic fragility of these countries, concessionality cannot be avoided. It will take prudent calculation for the Bank to play a supportive role, given its own exposure and the debt profile and export prospects of the countries. The accepted basis for qualifying external debt as sustainable is that it should be contracted at an average interest rate lower than the rate of export growth. This ratio allows a permanent current account deficit to be consistent with a stable debt/ratio export.

Against this background, management proposed that the five countries with severe economic difficulties (Bolivia, Guyana, Haiti, Honduras, and Nicaragua) should borrow only on the most concessional terms, that is, from the FSO. For the other six Group D countries (the relatively better-off Belize, Dominican Republic, Ecuador, El Salvador, Guatemala, and Paraguay), management proposed a fifty-fifty blend of ordinary capital and IFF resources. Based on historical lending growth rates, management estimated the need for an FSO lending program of $3.1 billion and an IFF lending program of $1.75 billion. The amounts allocated to each window were calculated to avoid a deterioration in the countries' external debt situations.

In contrast, the outgoing U.S. administration had proposed to restructure the concessional window, moving away from the FSO as a direct lender to an FSO II to provide interest support on OC loans. FSO II would be akin to the current IFF; the amount for concessional lending and technical assistance would come from new donor contributions, net income from the OC combined with existing net income from the FSO itself. But over the course of 1993, it became clear that the level of concessionality in this move was not sufficient to protect the Bank's portfolio from potential debt-servicing arrears among its severely indebted low-income countries.

The crux of the Eighth Replenishment negotiations hinged on these discussions. Virtually all FSO lending had to come from new contributions, as the Bank had almost exhausted its ability to raise concessional resources internally. Similarly, the Bank's ability to generate more IFF reserves from FSO earnings and reserves was stretched to the limit. The initial amount proposed by management was far from acceptable to the non-BMCs. One billion dollars in funds was finally raised with contributions from the nonregional non-BMCs, in particular from Japan. Coupled with reflows it will allow a lending program of about the same size as the Seventh Replenishment, but still $1 billion below management's proposal. The FSO facility will be made available only to the five poorest, least-developed BMCs: Bolivia, Guyana, Haiti, Honduras, and Nicaragua, and to the Caribbean Development Bank for on-lending to non-IDB members.

This is a doubtful solution because net resource flows on grants from other sources and bilateral loans have already begun to decline. New borrowers such as the former Communist countries claim part of a dwindling supply of concessional resources. The IDB is the only official source that is expected to have positive net flows in the years ahead, but they may not be sufficient to avoid a deterioration in the external debt situation of the severely indebted low-income countries. A debt reduction facility has not been discussed, nor has a new window akin to the Fifth Dimension at the World Bank to help the poorest countries repay loans contracted at nonconcessional terms. Debt reduction measures for Nicaragua, Honduras, and Guyana, whose debt indicators are not sustainable, should be considered the work of the country risk analysis unit.

## Operational Efficiency

The operational efficiency of the IDB was the subject of controversy for some years, and staff were aware of this problem. A 1982 study by the external review and evaluation office[4] of the Bank (IDB, *Evaluation Report on Delays*, 1982) found that deadlines for project completion were unrealistic. Only six of one hundred and sixty-two projects studied were completed within the original disbursement period stipulated by the loan contract (four to five years). During interviews among the staff, two points of view were expressed. One was that time schedules should be fixed in accordance with minimum time periods because "the shorter period puts the borrower under some psychological pressure"; the other, that execution periods should be realistic and adjusted to the knowledge of conditions and difficulties that surround projects. The latter would mean that projects need a six-to-eight-year period for disbursement, which is roughly the same as other development banks. Project teams have been authorized to recommend the disbursement period they believe is appropriate for their project. The highest concentration of incomplete projects was found in the transportation and public health sectors. When objectives were scaled down, the net expected benefits suffered. Efforts were made to be realistic. Some results were evident, but problems have not been eradicated.

Most problems occur in meeting contract conditions prior to first disbursement. A 1991 report (*Evaluation Report on Constraints*) on this problem studied projects approved between 1981 and 1987. It found that 40 percent of loans had postponed eligibility dates (that is, approval for first disbursement). Numerous setbacks were identified. Some delays were country-specific, which suggests that they could have been anticipated; others were sector-specific, suggesting that lessons could be extracted. The importance of the institutional capabilities of recipients was detected from the fact that global credit loans were the quickest to meet disbursement eligibility criteria. In contrast, rural integrated projects were among the slowest, averaging nearly nineteen months between Board approval and eligibility.

Acting on these findings in July 1991, the Board recommended the reduction and simplification of prior conditions, delegating to field offices the authority for determining compliance with general conditions, and providing more direct assistance to borrowers through technical cooperation or through the project preparation facility (PPF) to anticipate problems. The PPF, from which Group A and B countries were previously barred, was made available to them.

To a great extent, conditions prior to a first disbursement were used instead of quality control. As part of the discussions for the Eighth Replenishment, President Iglesias set up a taskforce to assess the overall portfolio management problems of the IDB. The six-man taskforce was headed by Moeen A. Qureshi, former interim prime minister of Pakistan and senior vice president at the World Bank. The report found that portfolio management was largely affected by the structure of governance. The Board's mistrust of management's ability to deal with BMCs led to a "culture of control," which has not allowed the Bank to be operationally flexible (IDB, *Managing for Effective Development*, 1993). Overregulation is pervasive and undermines efficiency.

The Board's time is heavily absorbed by day-to-day business, reviewing the minutiae of loan proposals and subsequent project reformulation and diverted away from substantial policy issues. "There are long standing tensions in the board-room between borrowing and nonborrowing member countries." Over the years, the Board has become "involved in matters which would ordinarily fall within management's responsibility" (IDB, *Managing for Effective Development*, 1993, 24). Board and management must trust each other to perform specific responsibilities.

Project reformulation without the need for Board approval would be a major step forward. Even if project design is flawless, conditions may change and projects need to be adapted. Quality can be enhanced as a project proceeds, but the need to resort to the Board for modification acts as a disincentive to be flexible vis-à-vis borrowers' needs as execution proceeds.[5]

Portfolio management is also handicapped by procurement guidelines more cumbersome than for any other MDB. Bidding thresholds are uniform, and there is no flexibility to adapt to local conditions or specific project needs. For example, even if it is obvious that no Canadian or Japanese firm will implement a small educational program in Ecuador, the international bidding procedures cannot be waived or adapted to the size of the operation. Procurement and bidding requirements are known to have caused delays. Loans cofinanced with the World Bank, for example, have been slow to get started for this reason.

Management responded quickly to these findings and presented an action plan to the Board in December 1993. Procurement guidelines will be simplified; there will be additional delegation to the field offices and a yearly presentation to the Board of the state of the portfolio.

Conditionality must also be streamlined. Programs with multiple conditions covering a wide number of agencies and policies and complex institutional designs are sometimes used to incorporate special donor country concerns that have marginal relevance to the project. Experience shows that overloading projects with conditionalities does not ensure that resources are used properly. Neither is project quality guaranteed. Unrealistic conditions may look good on paper and may be accepted by the borrower in financial need, but, if they cannot be met, these conditions will either have to be scaled down by the Bank or further tranches must be canceled later. Delays and unfinished programs strain relations and lead to low morale, both among officials in BMCs and IDB staff; many of these problems could have been anticipated and prevented.

It is important that the contractual conditions take into account the nature and individual features of the country and sector and that conditions be achievable. This is more crucial for social policy in the future than it has been in macroeconomic adjustment because executing agencies tend to be weaker than the treasuries in BMCs. It must be stressed that there is widespread recognition that many of the implementation problems can be traced to poor public management in the BMCs. The institutional factor cannot be exaggerated. The inability of the public sector to deliver and manage programs poses severe constraints on the successful execution of loans. Avoidance of overloading and attention to implementability must guide lending.

The above has implications for the skills-base of the Bank. The culture of control cannot reward professional judgment. Overemphasis is placed on compliance with each element of policy conditionality instead of a general review in which performance is assessed. There have been insufficient guidelines and training for a pragmatic conception of what constitutes compliance. Staff are trained to look for evidence of compliance instead of rewarded for their professional judgment. Flexible internal criteria are still being developed for dealing with cases in which conditions are not met as originally designed, as well as for separating soft from hard conditionality. The new criteria must change the balance from policing conditionality to assisting with implementation, for which technical assistance is badly needed. Skills must also be built where they are most needed—in the BMCs. The success of reforms depends as much on the content of policy as on the institutional capabilities in the BMCs. These need to go hand in hand. This is where the Bank must invest.

The culture of control has not only slowed down the process of loan development and approval but also affected execution. As stated in the TAPOMA report, "The Bank needs to move beyond the idea that successful projects result from strict application of Bank rules and procedures and enforcement of borrower compliance with conditions" (ibid. 11).

A related efficiency problem is the Bank's high cost of lending. Although these costs are comparable with other MDBs, it is clear that the IDB has become too big to be an efficient small-scale lender. It is important to analyze the potential duplication of functions between field offices and headquarters and see where these can be carried out with greater cost efficiency. In the short term, a division of labor must be sought with the subregional development banks whose coverage includes nearly all the small countries and many of the medium-sized countries. With training more tasks could be delegated to the BMCs themselves, particularly as the Bank moves to more staff-intensive operations.

## Notes

1. These are measured as disbursements less repayments of capital and interest and subscriptions to the Bank.

2. With Panama's emergence from nonaccrual status, net income reached $400 million in 1992. The profit was reaped by BMCs in the form of a waiver of the routine commitment fee as well as of the inspection and supervision fee on ordinary capital loans.

3. Currently, the IDB allocates all net income to reserves to boost its reserves to loan ratio. In 1987 the Bank established a policy that the reserves to loan ratio should be a minimum of 10 percent. In practice, reserves (defined as all reserves measured inclusive of currency adjustments and accumulated net income) have not fallen below 20 percent. At the end of 1991 they stood at 22 percent. All reserves together amounted to over $4.5 billion, which at the end of 1991 was equivalent to 25 percent of all loans outstanding; and 130 percent of loans outstanding to the largest borrower, Mexico.

4. The external review and evaluation office reported to the Board.

5. Likewise, doing away with standard disbursement periods to adapt these to genuine needs would avoid delays and would help reduce bureaucracy. Delays cost money to BMCs that are cost conscious due to tight fiscal policies.

# 8

# LOOMING DEVELOPMENT CHALLENGES FOR THE BANK

In 1991 the IDB regained its position as the leading official lending institution to Latin America. As Latin America moves into macroeconomic balance, the IDB is in a unique position to assist its BMCs in their renewed development efforts. The importance of a focused strategy and the need to build on the Bank's comparative advantage become vital.

The Portfolio Management Task Force drew attention to the effectiveness of IDB loans and to the determining influence of the governance of the Bank. It emphasized that excessive concentration on compliance with regulations acted to the detriment of development and sustainability. But it judged the Bank to be well positioned to deliver the new development agenda. For the sake of efficiency, the task force recommended delegation of responsibilities from the Board to management and from headquarters to field offices, a general reduction of bureaucratic procedures, and decentralization of authority. These changes would enable the Bank to become operationally flexible.

The assistance already provided to the development of the region also needs to be matched with a comprehensive, compelling, and coherent development strategy. The lending program evolved from a string of competing claims, resulting in mixed demands that have pulled the Bank in conflicting directions. The move into a sustainable level of lending to replace its four-yearly funding cycles should allow a more conducive atmosphere for long-term planning. At the same time, it places greater responsibilities on management for the design of a regionwide strategy.

The main challenges confronting Latin America today are related to the legacy of the debt crisis, the painful cost of adjustment, and the recovery of growth sustained by increased investment, innovation, productivity gains, and employment—"development from within"

(Sunkel 1993). In social terms, the alleviation of poverty and inequality is a priority. Crisis and adjustment in the 1980s meant that at the beginning of the 1990s the per capita income of the average Latin American fell to a level lower than that in 1980. Contributions from the private sector are vital. New growth requires adequate levels of capital accumulation, enhanced competitiveness, and energetic penetration of markets. The state must find a way to meet these priorities. It is not a question of turning back the clock to the dirigisme of earlier decades but of providing the conditions and environment for good governance.

## Poverty and Inequality

A priority in the looming development agenda is to tackle what is today recognized as the "social debt," the obligation to raise the living standards of the poorest and most vulnerable groups in society; in other words, to address the other side of the recessive adjustment policies adopted to meet external debt obligations.

Income inequities have been a shameful feature of the Latin American scene. The significant gains in social indicators during the three decades before the debt crisis were eroded during the 1980s. As adjustment proceeded, social investments were cut back and equity concerns relegated. Deterioration of social infrastructure, institutions, and systems of delivery is widespread. The traditional poor have been joined by a legion of new poor, those who lost their jobs as a result of restructuring and adjustment. The new poor swelled the ranks of the informal sector, becoming self-employed or working for microenterprises, raising the proportion of the poor from 41 to 47 percent of the population during the 1980s.

The IDB had a long-standing mandate to direct 50 percent of the benefits of its projects to low-income groups. In practice, there were serious obstacles in measuring the benefits of completed operations (see the discussion on the low-income target in Chapter 3). It is now obvious that more relevant is the adoption of a comprehensive approach centered around effective poverty reduction, either through projects of direct benefit to the poor or through operations that indirectly offer the poor economic opportunities.

The focus of new programs, both on humanitarian and social stability grounds, should be given to supporting the education, labor training, and employment needs of today's youth—the children who grew up during the lost decade. They constitute the human capital base on which future growth and poverty eradication rests.

The gender dimension is now acknowledged within the context of poverty reduction programs. The IDB has not made significant strides in this direction. The lack of systematic emphasis given to beneficiaries in project design omits gender differences that can affect the outcome of projects. Support for WID issues has been primarily through women-specific projects in the small projects program. Nearly half of the beneficiaries of the small projects program have been women, an average that has increased rapidly since 1990. However, the gender dimension must be incorporated into all programs and projects. Lack of access to training, nutrition, health, and education services has left women vulnerable to poverty.

The Bank is on its way to undertaking a social agenda. Over a quarter of commitments were earmarked for social sector lending in 1992 and nearly a third in 1993—the last two years of the Seventh Replenishment. As it enters the Eighth Replenishment, the IDB will expand its reach into poverty and equity issues, channel financial and technical cooperation resources for the design of appropriate policies, and improve the efficiency of social expenditures. One half of operations and 40 percent of total lending will be dedicated to social needs, equity, and poverty reduction. As its portfolio of investments in social sectors increases, new financing mechanisms must tailor repayment and grace periods to the long gestation periods of social projects and programs. Griffith-Jones et al. (1994) have recommended a diversification of lending vehicles, such as single currency windows and a U.S. dollar facility to reduce the cost of ordinary capital operations.

In all BMCs, the need is inescapable for structural reforms to promote greater mobilization and more efficient use of domestic resources. An attempt must be made to increase public revenues by broadening the tax base and making the burden more progressive. Nonetheless, the poorest BMCs will remain dependent on concessional funds. They are characterized by a reduced tax base and a larger share of the population living under the poverty line. The harshest aspects of poverty may be alleviated through emergency social funds and employment programs, such as those successfully tried in Bolivia and now replicated in El Salvador, Panama, and Guyana with IDB support.

In the more advanced countries, much can be achieved through fiscal policy and the mobilization of domestic resources. But a social and political consensus on providing public resources to fight poverty is a precondition for the transfer of resources. Given its mandate, resources, and technical skills, the IDB can contribute most to the struggle against poverty and inequality by putting political and intellectual muscle behind national efforts. Better information and analysis is crucial. The IDB should be encouraged to build a data base on vulnerable social groups. The system should be capable of producing annual reports on how every country is meeting the needs of its poor, including women and children. Research on the impact of policy reform on vulnerable groups should be actively promoted.

Griffith-Jones et al. (1994) recommend a new categorization of countries according to income and social indicators to facilitate lending for poverty and inequality. The current division into A, B, C, and D was last revised in 1975 when countries were adjusting to the oil shock. Poverty alleviation was not on the agenda. Unfortunately, the Eighth Replenishment agreement did not draw up a new classification—a proposal that merits attention if the IDB is to increase its share of lending to the poor.

This agenda must be consistent with the overall lending program so that poverty and equity issues do not remain encapsulated in social projects. In other words, the Bank should do its utmost to learn from its experiences with the low-income goal. Poverty efforts must become the central theme of the Bank's strategy in every country. Today, this should pose fewer difficulties than in the past. The electoral competition now existing in almost all BMCs means that grassroots demands can no longer be hidden from view.

Social reform is easier for the Bank today than during the Cold War competition when, for example, the Alliance for Progress was torn by conflicting ideals. The alliance tried to induce social reforms but at the same time supported backward and authoritarian regimes disinclined to democratic competition and social reform. It is not surprising that, in such a climate, many of the reforms of the period were viewed as politically intrusive. "More dialogue, more joint authorship of policy goals, and more ex-post conditioning leads to a more constructive and more congenial medium for leveraging pro-poor policy reform" (Lewis 1993, 4). Democratization has provided the Bank with a receptive atmosphere for its social agenda.

## The Private Sector

Most of the support provided to the private sector had historically been channeled through state-owned DFIs, which would direct (and subsidize) credit according to their own private sector objectives. But since the private sector became gradually recognized "as the engine of the economic growth process" (IDB, *Proposal for the Seventh*, 1989, 18), new and more dynamic ways to foster a competitive business environment have been sought.

Adjustment lending aimed to nurture the private sector, in particular, through the financial sector and investment sector loans and the public enterprise reform loans. The reforms have included improving supervision of banks and security markets, removing entry restrictions to financial markets, liberalizing credit and interest rates, and restructuring or privatizing DFIs.

The key issue on the Bank's agenda is whether to undertake direct lending to the recently privatized utilities. A distinctive feature of the IDB's mandate is the possibility granted by its Articles of Agreement of lending to the private sector without government guarantees. Nonetheless, since 1967 the IDB has required loans to other than national governments or agencies to be fully guaranteed. The United States, Mexico, Argentina, and Chile have suggested that the practice of requiring government guarantees be reconsidered for the large-scale, long-term investments needed in infrastructure and public utilities.

The high-level group appointed to examine the development of the private sector recommended that a program of direct lending be established but that the Bank's involvement be limited to projects that cannot be funded adequately by private sources. Chaired by Pedro Pablo Kuczynski, the group suggested an initial limit of 5–10 percent of total annual lending to be adjusted as needed. (Initial consultation with the markets had signaled that 3–5 percent would not affect the Bank's credit rating.) It also recommended that exposure be limited to a narrowly defined commercial risk.

A small new facility has been created since the Eighth Replenishment for direct lending to the private sector without government guarantees. It will be available only for large infrastructure and public utility projects providing services traditionally performed by the public sector. This lending cannot exceed 5 percent of commitments corresponding to the replenishment. The Bank's participation in each individual project cannot exceed 25 percent of total costs, or $75 million, whichever is less.

The limit falls short of the Kuczynski report; but it is seen as preserving the triple-A rating of Bank bonds and thus the lowest possible interest rate to borrowers. A higher limit would change the way the Bank does business. The higher risk on the Bank's portfolio would require appropriate loan-loss provisions and thus higher spreads on all loans; it would also require that the Bank be prepared to take on the discrimination of different risks—countries, projects, and institutions.

## The Inter-American Investment Corporation (IIC)

The IIC is also at a turning point. It began operations in 1989 as a window for direct lending, without government guarantees, to small and medium-sized enterprises. But its mission, to make long-term loans and equity investments in small enterprises that are costly and difficult to supervise, is complex and difficult. It has a limit of $10 million per operation. The large majority of its loans range from $2 million to $6 million. Its major stumbling block is that investments in this range are too large to reach small firms and too small to cover costs if they are undertaken directly instead of through intermediaries. Yet on-lending through financial intermediaries is limited to 30 percent of total funding, and additional limitations on project size do not allow opportunities to spread costs. The larger the project, the more opportunities exist to extend the cost over the volume and undertake small projects that are not as profitable.

The IIC faces cumbersome operating and policy guidelines coupled with limited delegation to management. Little flexibility to design specific operations is allowed. Modeled on the IFC, a much larger organization that is able to spread costs over voluminous operations, the IIC is not cost effective as presently structured.

Nonetheless, the IIC's track record proves that it has found a business niche. By mid-1993 it had approved loans for $374 million; the total cost of funded projects amounted to $1.7 billion. In other words, for every dollar invested by the IIC, $4 was provided by other sources. Exports from IIC-funded projects are estimated to average around $600 million a year. Job creation has approached 70,000 positions. Both the corporation and its clients in BMCs would benefit from flexibility to respond to market needs. A broader choice of eligible investments (in particular with respect to size) would strengthen the IIC.

By the end of 1993 all the IIC's initial resources had been committed. The United States proposed that either the IIC should be integrated into the Bank or IDB profits should be added to the capital of the IIC. The high level group did not agree. "Besides legal problems, such as the different memberships and purposes of both institutions, the principal purpose of the reinvestment of profits of the Bank is to maintain a strong balance sheet. . . . If the profits were to become too large, borrowing shareholder governments would no doubt insist on lower interest rates. . . . The capital structure of the two institutions, given their distinct purposes, should be kept separate. The subject is quite different from using a small part of Bank profits to support grants or soft loans to poorer countries. In principle there should not be a Bank subsidy to the private sector" (IDB, *The Inter-American Development Bank Group*, 1993).

### The Multilateral Investment Fund (MIF)

The MIF was established as part of the Enterprise for the Americas Initiative, with contributions totaling $1.3 billion. One billion dollars of these resources was provided in equal shares by the United States and

Japan; the rest came from nineteen other countries. The MIF has a mandate to improve the investment climate in the region as well as to increase financing available to the private sector.

The MIF has three separate facilities. Funds can be shifted among the three windows as required in consultation with donor governments. A technical assistance window provides grants to identify and implement policy reforms. A human resource facility (Window II) provides grants for labor restructuring, vocational education, and management training. Finally, a small enterprise development facility uses the Bank's expertise to develop a successful—if limited—program of support for small enterprises. It will provide revolving loans and equity investments to micro- and small enterprises and is meant to broaden participation of low-income groups, women, and minorities by enhancing business development and access to credit. This facility will also provide grants for institution building to support the financial services available to small firms. Based on the region's needs and the accelerated growth of microenterprises in all BMCs, the additional contribution of the MIF is relatively small. This means that the program must have a catalytic effect if it is to be useful.

As is obvious, the IIC, the MIF, and the Bank itself—through its global credit lines, small-projects program, and policy-based lending—offer complementary and at times overlapping channels to support the development of the private sector. The high-level group on private sector development recommended not merging identities. But tight coordination will be necessary, especially for small-project financing that needs access to other services and managerial, vocational, and technological training. Window II of the MIF is a focal point for such activities.

In summary the most important contribution that the IDB can make to nurture the private sector is to enable small firms to access credit at reasonable market rates and to compensate for the failures that often characterize capital markets. This will enlarge the business base in BMCs, enable a competitive environment to develop, and lay the foundation for renewed growth. In addition, private sector initiative requires a hospitable environment, and this requires the provision of public goods—physical infrastructure, social services, and efficient government administration ("good governance") (Culpeper 1993). These are still sorely lacking in most BMCs.

## Regional Integration and Cooperation

Regional integration is a central tool in the effort to compete globally. The revitalization of regional integration in the 1990s plays a direct role in adjustment and in the new growth strategies. In contrast to the

1960s when integration was viewed as an extension of import substitution, today integration is oriented toward the outside world. In addition, new varieties of integration incorporate donor and borrower regional members, NAFTA, and post-NAFTA, possibly encompassing the whole Western Hemisphere.

The IDB was a natural vehicle for promoting regional integration, but the historical record has been disappointing, for reasons beyond the control of the Bank. Before the external debt crisis erupted and regional integration collapsed, about 12 percent of lending was categorized as serving regional energy, transportation, and communications projects as well as technical assistance. The infrastructure suffered damage from the fiscal crisis of the 1980s. Substantial investments are required to expand, modernize, and maintain facilities. Much remains to be done to provide for regional physical integration. In addition to investments, assistance for design consistency or compatible regulatory frameworks to facilitate interconnection is also required, particularly in transportation and energy projects.

A reinvigorated Bank has engaged its regional members in discussions and research on a free trade area covering the Americas. With the end of civil strife in Central America, the Bank was entrusted by the presidents of Central America and Panama to chair a regional consultative group for Central America. With the participation of other international financial institutions, aid agencies, and donor countries, the group has a mandate to focus on integration issues. It considers projects and activities that are regional in nature with the active participation of the Federation of Private Sector Entities from Central America and Panama.

The new market-oriented policies open other activities and opportunities with the growing participation of the private sector: regional programs oriented toward technological modernization, assistance in the organizational and marketing aspects of companies, and the provision of marketing and financial services to enhance productivity. As integration proceeds, BMCs will need currency-clearing mechanisms and intensive assistance to update and harmonize regulations on commercial, environmental, labor, and investment sectors.

At the moment regional integration is proceeding as a bottom-up process. The Bank's role should be to provide a helping hand. The IDB should help countries make their haphazardly emerging integration schemes more compatible and consistent with each other. Much of this activism was prompted by the idea of a hemispheric free trade area; a good deal of the optimism is not warranted.

While the agenda of hemispheric integration takes shape, the Bank must build up its capacity to anticipate economic adjustments, and it must be prepared to help with adjustment assistance. Adequate attention will have to be paid to the prospective losers from the process of adjusting to free trade. The Bank will have to take precautions to ensure that regional free trade is compatible with its social agenda and with the antipoverty efforts of borrowing countries, so that the failures of the past to reach low-income beneficiaries are not repeated. Bottlenecks in regional physical infrastructure need IDB involvement in the immediate future.

## Role of the State and Institution Building

The economic collapse during the debt crisis left Latin America dependent on the policy advice of the donor community, "leading to an historically unprecedented explosion of conditionality" (Killick 1989). One cannot object to performance criteria to ensure that assistance is used for the right purposes. The effectiveness of projects is crucially affected by the quality of the policy environment into which it is introduced. A chief reason for policy-based lending was that many of the projects were failing, not because of design flaws but because the policy environment was eroding returns and undermining the expected impact on development. Problems associated with sound macroeconomic policies have been addressed.

But a new set of problems has emerged. Public sector capacity to develop and execute projects has been stunted by the 1980s crisis. Moreover, sentiment against the public sector is widespread and not unfounded. It stems from the overregulation, the inefficiency, and the lack of accountability of the governments in most BMCs. If the state is a fiefdom of rulers and unable to curb the power of vested interests, the potential of the public sector to provide institutional checks and balances cannot be realized. A good case can still be made for substantial deregulation and decentralization in most BMCs. Local ownership ranks high as a positive factor in the struggle for development. The essential issue with regard to the state is not its size but rather its administrative capacity and its ability to navigate among competing claims.

But in the conjunction of these two trends, the explosion of conditionality and the low administrative capacity in BMCs, lies a dilemma. Both programs and projects rely equally on policy content and on the institutions that are in charge of carrying them out. The final outcome of projects will be as good or as bad as the available management skills in BMCs. Yet administrative capacity is the weak link in countries south of the Rio Grande, and it is one that can be built only gradually.

The Bank needs to pay urgent attention to the administrative burden placed on executing agencies. Negotiations on lending programs are increasingly complex, and conditionality is wide ranging. The result is that scarce administrative resources are spread too thinly to achieve basic development objectives. This will be an even more important factor in the future as the Bank becomes increasingly involved with institutions in charge of social and environmental poli-cies—typically weaker than the treasuries in charge of macro policy. A great deal of the effectiveness of Bank operations will hinge on whether conditionality is well designed, flexible, sensitive, and feasi-ble.

The dearth of sound and efficient institutions throughout the region has several possible solutions. Loans for institution building and technical assistance need to be considered systematically. The improvement of staff selection, training, and skills in public agencies must be given increased attention. At the same time, the design of lending programs needs to be simplified. Although all development problems are related, a project cannot solve them all at the same time. The question of development impact cannot be solved by widening the assortment of issues on the agenda. On the contrary, non-BMCs should be aware that an overloading of the Bank's agenda is at odds with the capacity of national institutions. Jorge Quiroga verbalized a widely held view when he said in 1992 that he liked the way the IDB has operated with decentralized authority, but that it should come with the flexibility for rapid change. When a country begins health or education programs and has to send the proposal to Washington five times to get them approved, he suggested, it spends more money on faxes than on the projects themselves.

All IFIs are asked today to be more accountable, directly to their member governments and indirectly to their parliaments and their cit-izens. The IDB is preparing a comprehensive disclosure policy, which, as in other IFIs, assumes that, in the absence of a reason for confiden-tiality, information will be released.[1] An inspection panel will, in addi-tion, investigate allegations by affected parties that the Bank failed to apply correctly its own operational policies. The new evaluation office will also contribute to the transparency of the Bank by undertaking independent evaluations of policies and programs.

In parallel with the institutional renewal, democratic renewal has brought the development agenda back into balance. It has incorporat-ed fresh concerns about the social, economic, and gender inequalities in the region. It has allowed new means for delivering reforms. When beneficiaries participate in the formulation and implementation of goals, sustainability is more likely. Grassroots participation and democratization entail more than a periodic visit to the polls. The IDB supports good governance today by encouraging not only the mod-ernization of the executive arm of government but also by supporting the institutional renewal of the judiciary system and legislatures in BMCs. This achievement deserves high marks, but the delivery of these programs requires thought and new skills at the Bank. It can not, as when undertaking policy-based loans, delegate them to a "wiser" institution.

All told, the Inter-American Development Bank plays the lead role in setting the regional development agenda, establishing norms for confronting problems, and fixing priorities for action. By consistently focusing its attention on these, it will be able to inspire and support national efforts. It will have to do this not only by spending money or imposing conditions on its lending but also through active communication with the region and its leaders. The potential contribution of the IDB far exceeds the capital it can provide.

## Note

1. With or without a formal disclosure policy, IDB documents have circulated widely outside the institution.

# BIBLIOGRAPHY

## Sources Other Than IDB

Calvo, A., and L. Tomassini. *Una Decada de Lucha.* Mexico: Fondo de Cultura Economica, 1970.

Calvo, G., L. Leiderman, and C. Rheinhart. "Capital Inflows and Real Exchange Rate Appreciation in Latin America: The Role of External Factors." *IMF Staff Papers* (Washington, D.C.) 40, no. 1 (March 1993).

Canadian International Development Agency. *The Financial Viability of the Inter-American Development Bank.* Ottawa, 1992.

Cardoso, Eliana, and Ann Helwege. *Latin America's Economy: Diversity, Trends and Conflicts.* Cambridge: MIT Press, 1992.

Cassen, R., et al. *Does Aid Work?* Oxford: Oxford University Press, 1987.

Commission on Development and Environment for Amazonia. *Amazonia without Myths.* IDB/UNDP/Amazon Cooperation Treaty, 1992.

Culpeper, R. "Crossroads or Cross-Purposes: The Inter-American Bank at 31." Briefing B-25. Ottawa, Ontario: North-South Institute, 1990.

Culpeper, R. "The Regional Development Banks." Background paper, Bretton Woods Commission, Ottawa, Ontario: North-South Institute, 1993. Mimeographed.

Dell, S. *The Inter-American Development Bank: A Study in Development Financing.* New York: Praeger, 1972.

Griffith-Jones, S., et al. *An Assessment of the IDB Lending Programme.* Sussex: Institute of Development Studies, 1994.

Iglesias, E. *Reflections on Economic Development: Toward a New Latin American Consensus.* Washington D.C.: Inter-American Development Bank and Johns Hopkins University Press, 1992.

Inter-American Dialogue. *Convergence and Community: The Americas in 1993.* Washington D.C.: Inter-American Dialogue, 1992.

Kappagoda, N. *The Multilateral Development Banks: Volume 2, The Asian Development Bank.* Boulder, Colo.: Lynne Rienner, 1995.

Killick, T. *A Reaction Too Far: Economic Theory and the Role of the State in Developing Countries.* London: Overseas Development Institute, 1989.

Latin American and Caribbean Commission on Development and the Environment. *Our Own Agenda.* IDB/UNDP, 1990.

Levinson, J. "Multilateral Financing Institutions: What Form of Accountability?" Washington, D.C., 1992. Mimeographed.

Lewis, J. *Pro-Poor Aid Conditionality.* Overseas Development Council, Policy Essay No. 8. Washington, D.C., 1993.

Lustig, N. "Equity and Development." In O. Sunkel (ed.), *Development from*

   *Within: Toward a Neostructuralist Approach for Latin America*. Boulder, Colo.: Lynne Rienner, 1993.

Meller, P. "A Latin American Reassessment of the Role of International Financial Institutions." Paper presented at the Conference on the International Monetary and Financial System: Developing Country Perspectives. Sponsored by the Group of Twenty-Four, Santiago de Chile, 1994. Mimeographed.

Mosley, P. *Aid and Power: The World Bank and Policy Based Lending*. London and New York: Routledge, 1991.

O'Connell, A. "La deuda externa de los países de América Latina y los organismos internacionales de financiamiento." 1989. Mimeographed.

Ortiz Mena, A. "The Participation of the Inter-American Bank in the Economic Development of Latin America." Speech, banking meeting, Dubrovnik, 1979.

Please, S. *Sector Adjustment Lending and the Inter-American Development Bank*. IDB Occasional Paper No. 1, 1989.

Reichman, J. H. "Implications of the Draft TRIPs Agreement for Developing Countries as Competitors in an Integrated World Market." UNCTAD Discussion Paper No. 73, November 1993.

Reid, G. *Shocks and Strategies: Jamaica and the Caribbean Development Bank*. Ottawa: North-South Institute, 1995.

Rudengren, Jan. *Middle Power Clout: Sweden and the Regional Development Banks*. Ottawa: North-South Institute, 1995.

Schwartzman, S. "Statement Before the Subcommittee on International Development of the Committee on Banking, Finance and Urban Affairs." U.S. House of Representatives, Washington D.C., April 28, 1994.

Sovani, M. A. *The Role of Regional Development Banks in the Integrative Process of Developing Countries: Case Study of the Inter-American Development Bank*. Ottawa: Norman Paterson School of International Affairs, Carleton University, 1980. Mimeographed.

Sunkel, O., ed. *Development from Within: Toward a Neostructuralist Approach for Latin America*. Boulder, Colo.: Lynne Rienner, 1993.

Tussie, D., and Mirta Botzman. "Sweet Entanglement: Argentina and the World Bank (1985–1989)." *Development Policy Review* 8, no. 4 (December 1990).

United Nations Development Programme. *Human Development Report*. UNDP, 1991.

U.S. House Committee on Foreign Relations. *The U.S. and the MDBs*. 93rd Congress, 2nd session, March 1974.

U.S. Treasury. *U.S. Participation in the Multilateral Development Banks in the 1980s*. Washington, D.C., 1982.

Wade, R. *Governing the Market*. Princeton, N.J.: Princeton University Press, 1990.

White, R. *Regional Development Banks: A Study of Institutional Style*. London: Penna, 1970.

Williamson, J., ed. *Latin American Adjustment: How Much Has Happened?* Washington, D.C.: Institute for International Economics, 1990.

World Bank. *Adjustment Lending: An Evaluation of Ten Years of Experience*. Policy and Research Series No. 1. Washington, D.C., 1989.

World Bank. *Adjustment Lending by Regional Development Banks and Selected Bilateral Donors*. Sec M92-1478, Washington, D.C., 1992.

World Bank. *Effective Implementation: Key to Development Impact*. Report of the Portfolio Task Force, Washington, D.C., 1993.

World Bank. *Poverty Reduction: Handbook and Operational Directive*. Washington, D.C., 1992.
World Bank. *Statement of Loans*. Washington, D.C., 1991.
World Bank. *World Development Report*. Washington, D.C., 1990.


## IDB Publications

*Agreement Establishing the Inter-American Development Bank*, 1988.
*Annual Reports*, 1970–1992.
*Assessment of the IDB Reorganization Structure*. Office of the Controller, June 1992.
*Basic Management Proposals on the Reorganization of the Bank*. Report to the Board of Executive Directors, 1989.
*Bolivia: Country Programming Paper*, January 1993.
"Economic and Social Progress in Latin America," *Annual Reports*, several issues.
*El BID en la Argentina*, 1979.
*Evaluation Report on Constraints in Meeting Loan Conditions Prior to First Disbursement*, RE-170, 1991.
*Evaluation Report on Delays in the Execution of IDB Financed Projects*, RE-106, 1982.
*Evaluation Report on IDB and Micro-enterprise: A Development Strategy for the 1990s*, RE-179, 1991.
*Evaluation Report on the Monitoring of Projects During Execution*, RE-165, 1990.
*Impacto de los acontecimientos económicos recientes en la clasificación de países del Banco*, GN-870-7, January 23, 1975.
*IDB and Microenterprise*, 1991.
*The Inter-American Development Bank Group and Private Sector Development in Latin America and the Caribbean*. Report by the High Level Advisory Group on Private Sector Development, March 1993.
*Internal Operations Evaluation System*, RE-197, 1991.
*Managing for Effective Development*. Report of the Task Force on Portfolio Management for the Inter-American Development Bank, October 1993.
*Mid-Term Report on the Seventh General Increase in Resources*, March 1992.
*Operational Guidelines*. Debt and Debt Service Reduction Facility, GN-1686-7, March 22, 1991.
*Preparing a New Inter-American Development Bank for the 1990s*. Report of the High Level Review Committee to the President of the IDB, 1988.
*President's Report to the Board on Bank Activities*, 1992, 1993.
President's speeches to the Board of Governors, 1990, 1991, 1992, and 1993.
*Proceedings*, Annual Meetings of the Board of Governors, 1970–1992.
*Proposal for an Increase in the Resources of the Inter-American Development Bank*, GN-626-1, April 1970.
*Proposal for an Increase in the Resources of the Inter-American Development Bank*. Report to the Board of Governors, AB-648, December 1978.
*Proposal for the Sixth General Increase in the Resources of the Inter-American Development Bank*. Report to the Board of Governors, AB-910, May 1989.
*Proposal for the Seventh General Increase in the Resources of the Inter-American Development Bank*. Report to the Board of Governors, AB-1378, May 1989.
*Proposal for Concessional Resources for the Eighth Replenishment*, GN-1763-9, February 19, 1993.

*Report on the Eighth General Increase in the Resources of the Inter-American Development Bank*, CA-341-1, November 19, 1993, and revised versions; AB-1683, April 12, 1994.

*Review and Evaluation System*. Update of Evaluation Report on IDB operations in the Education Sector, RE-83, August 15, 1978.

*Review of the Low Income Goal*. Interim Report to the Programming Committee, CP-141, rev. 1990.

*Revised Report of the Operations Task Force*, February 1989.

*Sectores Sociales, Marco de Referancia para la Accion, 1992–93,* 1991.

*Social Reform and Poverty: Toward a Comprehensive Agenda for Development,* 1993.

*Two Years of Sector Lending Operations Cofinanced with the World Bank.* Special Evaluation Report, 1991.

# INDEX

African Development Bank (AfDB),
5, 79, 111
Allende, Salvador, 23, 27, 42, 45
Alliance for Progress (United States),
3, 20, 41, 79, 104, 142
Andean Development Fund, 9, 99
Argentina, 123; capital shares, 28*tab*;
Convertibility Act (1991), 68;
development level, 7, 39; development strategy, 68–69; economic
growth, 69; external debt, 126;
gross domestic product, 69; in
Inter-American Investment
Corporation (IIC), 33*tab*; loans
from Inter-American
Development Bank (IDB), 7, 42,
43*tab*, 44*tab*, 57, 68–76, 104, 108,
124, 126, 131*tab*; low-income population in, 82; privatization in, 68,
69, 74, 130; trust fund establishment, 13*n4*, 19–20; voting power,
7, 22*tab*, 24*tab*, 28*tab*
Asian Development Bank (AsDB), 5,
56*n18*, 79, 111
Austria: capital shares, 28*tab*; in
Inter-American Investment
Corporation (IIC), 33*tab*; voting
power, 21, 22*tab*, 28*tab*

Bahamas, 21; capital shares, 28*tab*;
development level, 7; in Inter-
American Investment
Corporation (IIC), 33*tab*; loans
from Inter-American
Development Bank (IDB), 7,
43*tab*, 44*tab*; voting power, 7,
22*tab*, 26*tab*, 28*tab*
Baker Plan, 50, 57, 69, 121
Balance of payments, 4, 36, 37, 52

Banks, commercial, 36, 60, 70, 71, 129
Banks, multilateral development, 9,
50. *See also individual banks*
Banks, private, 51, 52, 107
Banks, regional development, 20;
country-specific lending, 10;
development effectiveness of, xiii;
historical perspective, 2–7; overlap with World Bank, 8–9
Banks, subregional, 9, 12. *See also
individual banks*
Barbados, 21; capital shares, 28*tab*;
development level, 7; exchange
rates, 97; in Inter-American
Investment Corporation (IIC),
33*tab*; loans from Inter-American
Development Bank (IDB), 7,
43*tab*, 44*tab*; voting power, 7,
22*tab*, 25*tab*, 26*tab*, 28*tab*
Belgium: capital shares, 28*tab*; contributions to Inter-American
Development Bank (IDB), 41; voting power, 21, 22*tab*, 28*tab*
Belize: capital shares, 28*tab*; development level, 7; loans from Inter-
American Development Bank
(IDB), 7, 133; voting power, 7,
22*tab*, 26*tab*, 28*tab*
Bolivia: capital shares, 28*tab*; concessional borrowing, 133; debt
shares, 8; development level, 7,
40; economic growth, 63–64;
Emergency Social Fund, 102, 111;
exports, 8, 63, 64; external debt,
127; gross domestic product, 64,
68; in Inter-American Investment
Corporation (IIC), 33*tab*; loans
from Inter-American
Development Bank (IDB), 7, 42,

155

# About the Book and Author

The multilateral banks are powerful forces in the international community, providing loans of more than $250 billion to developing countries over the last half-century. The best-known of these, the World Bank, has been studied extensively, but the "regional development banks" are little understood, even within their own geographic regions.

This book looks specifically at the policies and projects of the Inter-American Development Bank, which, like the other multilateral banks, is being criticized increasingly by grassroots organizations, environmental groups, and others.

Drawing on case studies, Tussie responds to some basic questions: Has the IDB in fact been an effective agent of development? Has it been a mere clone of the World Bank, susceptible to that agency's weaknesses, as well as its strengths? She also assesses the Bank's ability to take on the emerging challenges on the development agenda, including such issues as governance, military spending, and the need for gender-sensitive development strategies.

**Diana Tussie** is senior research fellow at the Facultad Latinoamericana de Ciencias Sociales (FLACSO) in Argentina. She is coeditor (with David Glover) of *The Developing Countries in World Trade: Policies and Bargaining Strategies* (Lynne Rienner, 1993).